T0157604

Lighting the Lamp Within

Illuminating the Path to
Greater Spiritual Awareness

Jyoti Sondhi

iUniverse, Inc.
New York   Bloomington

Lighting the Lamp Within
Illuminating the Path to Greater Spiritual Awareness

iUniverse books may be ordered through booksellers or by contacting:

iUniverse
1663 Liberty Drive
Bloomington, IN 47403
www.iuniverse.com
1-800-Authors (1-800-288-4677)

Because of the dynamic nature of the Internet, any Web addresses or links contained in this book may have changed since publication and may no longer be valid. The views expressed in this work are solely those of the author and do not necessarily reflect the views of the publisher, and the publisher hereby disclaims any responsibility for them.

ISBN: 978-1-4502-5528-8 (sc)
ISBN: 978-1-4502-5529-5 (dj)
ISBN: 978-1-4502-5530-1 (ebook)

Library of Congress Control Number: 2010912980

Printed in the United States of America

iUniverse rev. date: 09/14/2010

Contents

Acknowledgments

I am thankful to the Universe for the inspiration to work on this book and the ideas that have flowed through me.

I thank my Reiki teacher and wonderful friend, Sangeeta Jaggia, for initiating me into Reiki. That was really the beginning of this amazing journey. Her training and insights into Reiki were instrumental in opening me to higher energy vibrations. I have been particularly inspired by the way she has handled her own personal challenges in a very spiritually enlightened manner, dedicating her life to healing at physical, emotional, mental, and spiritual levels. I have found this to be an outstanding example of spiritual learning applied in a practical way.

I am grateful to my husband, Rajiv, for sharing my spiritual journey with me over the years and growing with me on the same path of discovery. In the early years of our marriage, he had a knack for being able to laugh at my ego trips without putting me down—something that proved very helpful for my spiritual growth. I have been particularly inspired by the absence of a strong ego and emotional baggage in his personality. I thank him for demonstrating to me a life of humility, unconditional giving, and compassion. He has given me a feeling of security and stability throughout our marriage. My spiritual journey has surely been facilitated by his unwavering support.

I also thank him for his extensive editorial contribution in the writing of this book.

Introduction

I still remember the wizened face of the temple priest very clearly. As I prayed at a crowded temple in northern India, sang collective hymns with the large crowd of devotees, with all the color and the noise, he took me aside and told me, "Every person's journey toward spiritual awakening is a personal and individual one. It can happen at any time, age and stage in life. All you need is to wake yourself up, open yourself to receiving blessings and spiritual guidance."

That was many years ago. These words stayed with me for a long time, though I was not sure exactly what he meant. I often reflected upon this comment and noted that many of us unwittingly do block out spiritual guidance as we go through our lives. Where was the time? We get caught up in our daily routines, or in resolving challenges that appear in our day-to-day lives. Our mind is preoccupied with acquiring material objects, or looking after them. For many too, status is a greatly desired acquisition. As a result, we don't find time to quiet the mind and get in touch with our inner self.

I have lived such a life too, for many years, until a kind of awakening turned my life around completely. What I learnt in this process, about my Self, where I am in my spiritual journey, and practical lessons in spiritual living, is what I want to share with you in this book.

Spiritually speaking, the turning point crept quietly into my life about ten years ago. I was introduced to Reiki (a form of alternative healing) almost by coincidence. When I went for my first Reiki session, it was not because I was seeking relief from stress or a healing for any specific health problem, but simply out of curiosity and at the urging of a close friend. Looking back, perhaps it was a case of Divine "coincidence," as it opened so many new doors for me.

During my early Reiki sessions, I saw people coming there to seek healing for physical or emotional problems. Many seemed to face difficult situations that they could not cope with in their personal lives, and seemed desperate for help. On the "healing-sharing" days at these sessions, one thing that struck me was that even the most stressed people left the room absolutely relaxed and composed. The energy in the room seemed to calm them. Their faces radiated a new hope!

I decided to get formally initiated into Reiki and continued to the third level. Every level of initiation took me to a different energy "vibration," but it was particularly after the third level that I felt and experienced a major shift deep inside myself. It was as if internally I had been pushed over by a big storm and thrown into a higher vibration—to a different elevation.

Reiki had a deep cleansing effect on me. For the first time, I learned about emotional cleansing, how to neutralize negative blockages through positive affirmations and creative visualization techniques. Emotional cleansing is important if one aspires to move up spiritually, as it helps remove blockages that have arisen from past resentments and regrets—blockages that many of us carry within us, consciously or subconsciously. My emotional cleansing triggered some physical reactions normally associated with illness, as if even at the physical level toxins were being released. However, I did not feel sick, tired, drained, or dehydrated. Instinctively I knew that what I was experiencing was cleansing, deep inside. Knowing *this* was in itself very comforting and reassuring.

I regarded my Reiki initiations as potential techniques for alternative healing, and did not think beyond that. I had no expectation of any outcomes. I was not waiting for any spiritual spark. In fact, I did not even know that there was a connection between the two. Looking back, I feel that I received spiritual awakening precisely because I did not block the flow of this blessing with any expectations or fears.

I did not fully understand this at the time, but I felt a kind of *merger* taking place inside me. One day, I felt that I had really *woken up*, as if something inside me had just *opened*. I started to feel very light and complete, and my inner world became calm and peaceful. I experienced intense feelings of gratitude and faith that seemed to blend with my very breath. Such inner refreshment and joy even brought tears at times. I felt like I was in a trance.

Around this time, I also started reading a wide range of books on spirituality. I read and I read! I feel that I was attracted to just the right books at just the right times, and each book took me to a different level of comprehension and experience. These books really validated how I was feeling. I did not realize at the time that what I was experiencing was in fact an *awakening*, or a kind of spiritual shift inside me. I was aware that the way I was feeling was not "normal." I associated this experience with my physical body adjusting to the cleansing from Reiki. It did not occur to me that ordinary people like me could realize spiritual awakening in this manner.

The more I read—and these were not religious books but more contemporary works on spiritual experiences and insights—the more I felt my feelings and experiences being validated. Sometimes, they brought visions and sometimes vibrations in my arms. And sometimes, goose bumps, because I could relate so clearly and in an experiential way with what some writers were saying in their books.

This was very important for me, as without these confirmations, I would not have even understood exactly what was happening to me. They confirmed, sometimes page by page, that I was having the experiences that spiritually aware people are likely to report. I began to realize that I had grown spiritually. This combination of energy tune-up and the wisdom in the books I read created a new idea of spiritually aware living for me.

All these together have transformed the way I deal with day-to-day challenges that all of us encounter as human beings. Gradually, my perspective on life changed. This new perspective has shaped my life and that of my family in a demonstrable way.

I began to realize and feel that many people who had come into my life had come for a reason—either to teach me or to learn something from me at a spiritual level. I started connecting the dots of my various past experiences—particularly the unpleasant ones—that had not made sense earlier. These made eminent spiritual sense now. I felt joyful at what I newly perceived.

I understood a bit more about human nature and how ego manifests in manifold ways, and holds us back spiritually. I learned to recognize the various facets of ego. I understood how emotional blockages control us, sometimes for a lifetime, and are usually a major hindrance to spiritual growth. I also began to understand creative visualization techniques and affirmations, applying them in my daily life, with some miraculous results. I understood the power of thought and how the Law of Attraction applies to our positive and negative thoughts. More importantly, I understood the potent power of prayer and gratitude to the Divine Source.

At some point, I sensed a new energy underlying all these aspects in my life. I felt vibrantly awakened inside.

After my awakening, the thought of death did not hold any fear for me. I did not have any more pressing questions and did not need answers for what happens at death, what happens after death, who are angels and who are spirits – none of these were important. It's as if all the questions had been answered for me. Besides, let's be honest: what would I gain by knowing the future, or knowing about what happens after death? How would that knowledge enhance my faith in the Divine Source or enlighten me as to how I should live this life? It was simply no longer relevant. When we live in the *now,* we do not need to worry about the future. Death is future beyond this life, and I did not need to know anything more.

I had found my answers and validations in the concept of "energy," a term that many writers use in the context of the Universe and Divinity. My sacred truth is that the higher the vibration of energy in our life, the closer we are to feeling and knowing and *being* the Higher Truth. The remaining puzzle is to understand how to reach and live at that higher energy vibration. And that is what I have tried to explain in this book.

Living in gratitude attracts more and more reasons to be grateful, because living in positive thinking attracts more positivity into our life. What more could anyone want on the worldly plane? Even today, I have no desire to know anything beyond what's present, as it is in the *present* that I can be aware of my feelings, my hidden fears, and my negativities.

It is in the present that I can control my thoughts and my mind; it is in the present that I can make my choices, make my affirmations, offer my prayers, and live in gratitude; it is in the present that I can breathe, and it is in the present that I can live and stay "awake."

After this awareness, I reached a stage in which I could not hold on to the information that was flowing through me. I felt that I would burst from the continuous flow of spiritual insights! I remember telling my husband one day that I felt the urge to write, as my head was whirling with all these new ideas. He introduced me to the idea of a blog. Lo and behold, before he got back from the office that very day, I had already started it and had blogged my first two pieces. When I first started writing in my blog, I had no idea that it would take the shape of this book. This idea developed only after many readers made appreciative and insightful comments on the blogged writings and discussions, and some suggested that I should reach a wider readership.

Last year when these inspirations came to me, I did not read any book on spirituality. I felt that such reading could interfere with my own flow of inspirations and guidance, and I wanted my writings to come straight from my heart and not get influenced by somebody else's work. The result is that I am able to share my experiences with all of you in very simple and easy-to-understand language, ever hopeful that you will enjoy and benefit from this as I have.

Even as I started expressing myself, the pieces of the jigsaw of my spiritual growth started to come together, and my whole journey made even more sense to me. I felt that another subtle shift had taken place in my spiritual growth.

After my awakening, I have looked at my experiences and the people who have come into my life—even if fleeting— in a whole new light, and through a different filter. I have reflected on many events and relationships in a different way. I have gleaned some nuggets from my journey that I believe you will find interesting and helpful. These did not come to me in a flash or in any sequential order. However, I have presented them in a collection of brief essays that are grouped thematically by sub-topics to help lay down some coherent building blocks for spiritual growth. You will find examples from my own life and the lives of people I know or have met, whose identities I have withheld to respect their privacy.

The essays in this book are based on inspirations that came to me as and when the Universe knew it was the opportune time for me to receive them. I gratefully received them, then lived them and applied them in my life. And this application of spiritual concepts, I believe, has given me a unique practical perspective on spiritual living from which I am guided to see and conduct my life. I call this my spiritual journey.

Many of us follow religious faiths and adhere strictly to the beliefs and practices that these faiths prescribe. Over the years I have been exposed to different kinds of religious practices in many countries. Yet I have found that religious practices often tend to focus on rituals and rigid dos and don'ts. However well intentioned and potent these rituals and moral prescriptions may be, I have found that blind adherence to them often prevents people from appreciating the true spiritual content of their religion. The deeper messages that underlie dogma and rituals sadly get lost, and many people are not even aware of this. I have met many God-fearing people and have wondered why anyone would follow a religion out of fear of the Divine. Does this fear not hold them back from exploring the depths of their own spirituality?

And so I have wondered—do religious beliefs and rituals encourage or hinder individual spiritual growth?

I have also read and pondered the interpretations of some ancient religious scriptures and the spiritual thoughts of some very eminent contemporary writers from around the world. I have often found them thought provoking and uplifting. They made me question many aspects of my life that I had earlier found puzzling. But truth be told, some parts of those discussions eluded me, left me reaching out for even more answers. The lucidly expressive language of some writers, though very appropriate to the context and beautiful to read, left me entangled in syntax sometimes. Spiritual concepts can at times be inherently abstract and difficult to grasp. I simply yearned for an experiential way of grasping this immense knowledge. What was I missing?

I felt that merely conceptual discussions on spirituality may not be easily understood and assimilated by the large majority of people I know—people who, like me, are ordinary people living ordinary lives and searching for some deeper meaning.

Then how do we bridge the gap of this "missing middle," between religious beliefs and conceptual theology? This is what I have tried to address in this book.

I am neither a journalist nor a writer by profession, nor indeed a spiritual authority of any note. I have lived a very ordinary life—as a daughter, a sister, a housewife, a mother and a language teacher. I continue to apply myself dutifully to many worldly activities and responsibilities in my life, quite like most people that I know.

I am sharing my personal insights with you, my readers, to help make you aware that if an ordinary person like me could be graced with this spiritual awakening, which has deeply affected the way I live, you can experience it too. I am now able to deal with day-to-day issues with a shift in perspective and equanimity that I find soothing. I do not have answers to all the questions that you may have about spirituality. However, I do hope to trigger some reflections in you, and hope they will help you in your own spiritual journey.

I am convinced that as we become aware of our own spiritual growth and awareness, each one of us will find his or her true purpose in life. This is a journey to personal fulfillment, born of a desire to fill the inner void that sometimes makes us feel lost and incomplete, a journey illuminated with a lamp that each of us can light within, bringing lasting peace and calm.

As you read this book, you can read the chapters sequentially, or dip into any particular topic that seems interesting on any given day. I have deliberately refrained from giving any prescriptive exercises for you to start applying the spiritual concepts. I believe that every one will be touched differently. But after each essay I have left space for you to note down your reflections. I would suggest that as you go through this book, take time to pause and reflect on any feelings and questions that arise in your mind. These reflections will form important guideposts in your spiritual journey.

Now that you have the book with you, know that it is not about *me*.

You were attracted to this book because you are ready to explore your own inner universe. If you see yourself reflected in any of the examples or essays, try to be aware of any defense mechanisms that you may trigger in yourself, as that would actually be a moment of healing, or when your spiritual growth may begin, or resume.

This book is really about *you* taking control of your life in a spiritual way, with a deliberate shift in perspective. It is about you lighting your spiritual lamp and living in its glow.

Part One

HUMAN NATURE

Our Unconscious Hurdles

1
Perceptions—our inner filters

"If the doors of perception were cleansed everything would appear to man as it is, infinite."

William Blake

With all the communication skills and tools that we have developed through the millennia, sometimes I wonder if we have really got it right. That is, do we understand each other increasingly better? More important, do we understand *ourselves* better, deep down inside?

During my training as a language teacher, we were rigorously taught to carefully read texts for comprehension. We were encouraged to understand the text globally, then to read between the lines, and finally to read *beyond* the lines. My husband tells me that this technique of reading "beyond the lines" and searching for hidden agendas was standard fare in corporate management-training programs that he has attended.

This technique, appropriate as it may be for learning a language, does get us into trouble when applied in our everyday lives. It seems to me that many people have stopped reading and understanding one another at face value. On the contrary, we attempt to read beyond what others are actually saying or implying—to read *into*. A simple declarative statement is not just understood at its own, straightforward level, but at far-flung removes. The intentions of the speaker are not just analyzed, but guessed, judged, turned and twisted every which way, so that they can come out looking malicious when there was no such intent.

I am sometimes shocked to see how people can take innocuous remarks and make them look ugly in their own minds. A chain of thoughts then follows, based on habitual prejudices, each thought justifying and propping up the previous one and leading to a totally different conception than what was initially intended. We've all seen the problems that a guileless soul may encounter when offering his point of view. Each misinterpretation of his words, some intentional, must be clarified and denied! Such miscommunication drains time and energy, as all parties try to resolve their differing views. What's worse, people who read beyond the lines may discuss and gossip about what they *thought* was meant or intended. This too can be quite a waste of their time and energy. On both sides, the mind is busy churning and cranking out thoughts, each thought clamoring for its very life—and hours wasted trying to figure out what was really meant and who is "right."

Does any of this sound familiar? We create so many problems because of this common human trait. It can ruin loving relationships and kill business deals. If people did not judge one another so quickly, based on their distorted perceptions, life would be simpler and less complicated. Having suffered some nasty experience in the past, we can unknowingly allow that to skew our ongoing perceptions, thereby contaminating the lives of many people around us. We can get stuck in the sticky web of complications; trying to extricate ourselves from them, we sink ever deeper. Why does this happen?

It seems we perceive the world through the filters of our own past experiences and fears of the future. Since each person's experiences and fears are different, each one of us is likely to interpret the same situation in different ways. Unique fears and experiences shape unique filters of perception, which can generate serious flaws in our personalities.

The story line in the movie *Doubt* is a good example of what I mean. Gossip started by a teacher about a colleague's behavior toward an adolescent student feeds doubt into the principal's mind about that teacher's intentions. Her doubts quickly change to increasingly strong suspicion about what may be the teacher's impropriety. In spite of the fact that there is no foolproof evidence, this perception is amplified, justified, and validated in her mind. She eventually confronts the accused and, despite denials, decides to apply sanctions. It does not occur to her at all that her accusations could be totally baseless. Only after the suspected colleague is forced to resign from his job at the school does she come to realize that he was, quite possibly, completely innocent and simply helping a child to cope with domestic issues. At that point, her doubts turn inward to her own judgment, leading to remorse and regret.

Such behavior may seem very familiar to many of us. Taking events and people at face value almost sounds old-fashioned these days. The possibility of intrigue—never mind that it's often imagined—can be so fascinating! It seems that we do not trust people enough, and suspect almost everyone of an unsavory motive behind all that's said or done.

If we lead our lives based on totally subjective perceptions, it can do much damage to our relationships and us.

Let's take another example. You telephone a friend and he does not pick up the phone. Your mind starts imagining all kinds of reasons: "I hope he's not angry with me! What did I say or do that keeps him from answering the phone? Does he think I'm boring?" Very quickly, your mind starts painting scenarios of personal rejection, and nothing looms larger than the scary thought of being ignored by your friend. It finally turns out that he was simply busy taking his sick mother to the hospital just at the time you called. When you find this out later, you feel silly for all that mental and emotional anguish, simply because of your insecure fears of being unloved and of abandonment!

When fears are founded on misperception, you might take it out on others, lashing out for no fault of theirs, thereby frustrating and angering everyone involved. The situation can get even more intricate, with others trying to figure out *their* perceptions of the reasons for your behavior, based of course on the "creative" filters of their own minds. When reality dawns and our doubts are dispelled, we are caught in a pattern of guilt and remorse. Guilt and remorse eat us from within and further muddy our perceptions of our world and relationships.

What does this have to do with spirituality?

We may not realize it, but these inner filters, through which we interact with people, generate and nurture negative emotions, which in turn deplete our energy levels. They are building blocks of emotional baggage that obscure our own inner Divine nature from others as well as from ourselves. A straightforward person is more reliable and trustworthy. He does not read beyond or "between the lines" of what his interlocutor is saying. He does not compulsively analyze and judge others' statements. His mind refuses to think along those lines. In this way, he avoids the mental baggage that is an obstacle to spiritual awakening.

Adopting or maintaining this stance through life does offer practical challenges, in particular when we interact with people who prefer to operate through perception filters. That said, my experience has been that eventually, trust inspires trust, compassion inspires compassion, and love inspires love. As a result of this state of mind, I have often been able to draw out similar positive energy vibrations in others and thus attract their positive qualities to me. It has been very pleasing to find others, knowingly or unknowingly, change their behavior toward me. Transparency in relationships and communication is indeed a great energy balancer!

I have trained myself to see people around me simply operating at different vibrations of energy and levels of spiritual growth. The energy exchange in any interaction is at a subconscious level and can be very subtle. Yet, I have seen the beauty and the potency of this energy exchange. It strengthens the Self by bringing up soul qualities in others, thus removing a key hurdle in spiritual evolution.

My Reflections

....
....
....
....
....
....
....
....
....
....
....
....
....
....
....
....
....
....
....

2

The predicament of being judgmental

"If you judge people, you have no time to love them."

Mother Teresa

When my teenage daughter once told me that she had a friend who was gay, I recall that my immediate reaction was to feel very disturbed. Coming from a conservative family in India where this matter was taboo, I just could not accept that my daughter would make friends with a gay person. In spite of her saying that he was a wonderful person and a good friend, I had this nagging discomfort that I could not quite rationalize.

It was only later in life that I realized, upon reflection, that I had unfairly judged someone I didn't even know and had never met. What made me reject that youngster in my mind? Who gave me the authority to judge another person? One could argue that in life we do need to judge, or at least evaluate, people with whom we transact business or interact on a daily basis. But must this be in a critical way of putting someone down, even if it happens only in our mind? I realized that it was my ego that was not allowing me to accept people who were simply different. I viewed *my* "right" as *the* "right," and everybody else's as invalid—a notion that was totally ego-driven.

In a social gathering or an informal meeting, it is interesting to see how much attention we devote to "scoping out" and silently judging others. We judge them on the basis of their looks, their education and knowledge, their social status, their habits, clothes, and so on. Even if we don't always articulate these impressions, or are not aware of how the mind is indulging in this exercise, such judgments often creep into our minds.

Not only do we judge people; we often go so far as to label them! Whether we're dealing with friends and associates, passersby, or even our own children, we may find ourselves mentally labeling people, and using the most astonishing adjectives. We relish in giving them names—dolt, bore, creep, fatty, anorexic…mentally turning up our nose at them. In putting them down in our own minds, we hold damaging thoughts against them. But you know what? Such thoughts are no other than our negative energies that can't help but "leak out." We may not always realize this, but what we are secretly thinking about others might show up in our own behavior, in our conversations and in unspoken ways such as our facial expressions. And if that does not happen, at the energy level, many people can very quickly sense internal biases in people around them.

When we criticize someone, we may feel superior. Our comments can undermine that person, and lower his or her self-esteem. And that gives power, temporarily, to our power-hungry egos. This is a way to assume external power and feel good, albeit in a twisted way, about ourselves.

During my training as a teacher, we were always told never to use the words *never* and *always* (There I go again!) when talking to a child. So instead of saying, "You never do your homework"—which could attract the response, "I did it once three years back," or "You are always late"—which could lead to, "I was early four months back," we were urged to use *often* or *sometimes*. We were taught to speak positively and not be critical or judgmental in our dealings with children.

Yet, I found myself still being critical with my own children. I tended to label them in my mind instead of focusing on the behavior that needed correction.

When we label or categorize others in any way, we put them down and we drain them, after which they may feel impelled to re-energize themselves—sometimes by doing exactly what we just did to them.

They seek to replenish themselves, get soothed and energized, using the same tools to obtain external (false) power.

As mentioned earlier, when we judge or criticize someone, we wrongly deduce that we are better, or that we know better. The irony here is that we notice only those negative qualities in others that in fact scream for healing in ourselves. So when we say that someone is jealous, greedy, or angry, if we look honestly inside ourselves we will see that those are the very attributes in our own personalities that need awareness and change.

Many contemporary writers on spirituality focus in this regard on the Law of Attraction. The notion here is that because "like attracts like," we will keep attracting circumstances and people with certain qualities, even if we consider these negative, as long as they are present in ourselves and need our attention. No change will occur in our lives until we become aware of these qualities and make a conscious decision to change them. Unpleasant encounters are, in fact, reminders from the Universe of the healing that needs to take place within us. These are the times for us to become aware of our negative qualities, and break the flow of energy that feeds them.

You may have heard the saying that when we point an accusatory finger at someone, four fingers of the same hand are pointing back at us. How true this is! "It's only human," you might say, to ignore our own weaknesses and vices while projecting these faults onto others. Yet it is in our larger interest to take these as reminders from the Universe, that when we see that proverbial speck in someone else's eye, we need to work four times harder to remove the plank from our own!

To evolve spiritually, we have to understand—not just understand, but *feel*—that all human beings are spiritual beings, each one precious and indispensable, and that nobody is superior and nobody is inferior. People are just different, each one expressing Life in a unique way. Everyone is the way he or she is meant to be. Everyone is in the *right* place for the exactly right experiences and lessons that he or she needs. There are no mistakes in the Universe, for the Universe is truly perfect.

Once I understood this *Truth,* my approach to people changed. When I note differences in people, I stay neutral in my feelings and thoughts. I have become less judgmental and more compassionate.

My Reflections

....
....
....
....
....
....
....
....
....
....
....
....
....
....
....
....
....
....
....
....

3
From boredom to "inspire-dom"

"Boredom is a feeling that everything is a waste of time; serenity, that nothing is."

Thomas S. Szasz

"I'm bored."

How often do we hear this statement? When my children were young, bubbling with energy as children often are, I used to hear it all the time at home, never mind the toys, computer games and video games!

If I now think about it, what really is boredom? What exactly do we mean when we say we are bored? The dynamics of the mind are such that it needs to process a continuous flow of thoughts. So when we say we are bored, essentially the mind is looking for new things with which to occupy itself. It needs more food for thought. At any given time, note how the mind skips from one thought to another. In the flick of a second, one thought leads to another, and another, until our thoughts control us. All the mind needs is a trigger. When it finds one, it takes charge, and the rest of our life can seem beyond our control.

I am reminded of a famous poem, "Leisure," by William Henry Davies, that we read in school: "What is this life if, full of care, we have no time to stand and stare." In reality, it seems we are scared of having extra time on our hands, and the thought of an idle mind intimidates us. In my Metro commute, I often notice many faces peering into iPods or newspapers. Never an idle moment, never a sign of stillness to be seen! Sometimes we engage in more and more activities to pass our time, never suspecting that in fact, time is passing *us* by!

We keep chasing time, but whenever we want to catch it, it slips right through our fingers. We experience and "accomplish" much more than our parents and grandparents did. However, in our own estimation, we still fall short. With this come frustration and the feeling of not achieving enough. But do we really need to do quite so much? Why do we keep increasing the number and complexity of the things we want to experience and accomplish in life? Can we not sacrifice some activities so that we can get a little quiet in our life and smell the roses?

I asked my husband once what he "does" in the gaps between our conversations. He said that his mind often wanders from one topic to another—work issues, children, house chores, golf game—there is just so much happening in life, he says! Does that sound familiar? I suggested to him that in those gaps he could practice stillness, and stop the mind, even if it is for short intervals. These are precious moments that could be utilized to practice stillness, to go within and get connected to the True Source. And that would be productive "use" of his time!

Children these days keep themselves busy, quickly getting bored or jaded after the initial desire to possess or do something has passed. Their short attention span is well researched and documented. Not only that, they expect their parents to continuously seek out new gadgets and activities to blast them out of their boredom. Now here is the catch! When parents themselves say that *they* are bored and do not know what to do with their spare time, their children unknowingly adopt this attitude, little knowing that there could be options. If somehow parents could demonstrate staying still from time to time and get comfortable with that state of stillness, their children would learn to accept that as normal. The regular practice of stillness from a very young age can be a valuable training for long-term well-being.

In times now forgotten, "snail mail" used to take its sweet time in reaching its destination, and then the letter-writer would usually have to wait even longer to get back a reply. This not only taught us patience but also gave us "thinking time" to peacefully find solutions to our day-to-day problems. Today, Internet and emails make life go much faster, and text messages have greatly expedited the numerous decisions we have to make in a short span of time. These days, people who are "on the go" may well be thinking, "I don't even have time to die!" With this frenetic lifestyle, we may be dying anyway, spiritually speaking.

Some like to compensate for this lifestyle with designated time spent on discussions and readings on spirituality. For many years my husband would spend time every weekend on reading discussions on the Holy Geeta. Though undoubtedly such time is well spent, I question if it adequately substitutes for the time spent "within." If we attempt to understand the subtleties of the Divine only with our intellect, would we not fall short? Consider this: the intellect is inherently a finite instrument, and a creation of the infinite Divine. Although it is a useful tool in this journey, after a certain point the busy mind can become an impediment to spiritual growth. The truth is that only when the mind is *still* can we get glimpses of the Divine and *feel* the inspirations. Only then are we fully open to the inflow of Grace.

The challenge is how to use this limited human instrument, the mind, to support us in our quest for spiritual growth. For this, we need to still the mind from time to time. Quiet moments, even if occasional and fleeting, will gradually attune us to higher vibrations. The way to do this is to stop constantly giving the "trigger" of stimuli to the mind. We need to convert our boredom—which is little more than muted tension—with "inspire-dom."

This is not easy to do for many of us. It is just natural for the mind to be busy all the time. Thoughts seem to flow with a mind of their own! Coaxing the mind to shut off completely and still itself is indeed a challenge for many people. A technique that works well for some is to replace random thoughts gently, *without force*, with a single word, a thought, or a feeling. This is the concept on which 'transcendental meditation' is based upon—transcend the mind and feel the Divine within! My approach has been to divert my mind with simple affirmations, thus replacing the flow of myriad thoughts with a single thought—"I am calm; I am in peace." This diminishes the mind's restlessness and brings about stillness. After my awakening, I have forgotten what boredom is. There were times when getting caught in a traffic jam was an incredibly frustrating experience for me. I would constantly look at the time, which just did not seem to pass. Now, I can spend hours waiting at an airport or in traffic without getting angry or upset. My mind automatically goes toward prayers and accesses the calm inside. Boredom does not exist there.

What may be perceived as boredom by the person who is more or less locked into the material world can be a period of great inspiration to artists, poets, and writers, for whom creating art is a spiritual connection. For those who are consciously connected to the Divine Source, it is a period of spiritual renewal and growth. It is a time and space to be still, to be aware, and to experience union with the Divine.

My Reflections

4
The art of giving

"To give without reward, or any notice, has a special quality of its own."

Anne Morrow Lindbergh

It has been said that as long as we are in a position to stretch out our hand in a gesture of giving, we should feel blessed.

We can only give what we have. That is stating the obvious. So a wealthy person may not have time, but he does have financial resources to give; a retired person may not have money, but he has free time to give to others. And even when we have neither resources nor time, offering a few words of love, encouragement, and energy can be a gift. Focused listening and attention to someone in need can be gratefully received too!

Let's consider the example of a very simple gesture of giving that we often don't pay much attention to. Many of us go through a period in life in which someone tries to make us feel small and insignificant. Somehow, it "gets to us," leaving us feeling ignored, devalued, and dejected. It may happen anywhere—at big parties or in a group meeting at work, where we do not know anyone, or where people have formed their own little cliques, ignoring the glaring fact that we could also be included in their conversations. We all know how uncomfortable that feels at the receiving end! One thing that I have learnt in such situations is the power of a friendly smile—an act of simple acknowledgment of someone else's presence and existence. We may not know the other person, but just a simple greeting or a smile or an eye-to-eye contact can make that person's day. A smile costs us nothing and pays back with the warmth and inner joy it generates. A smile is infectious, as everyone who sees it "catches it," leading to a chain of lighthearted people all around. Try it out next time during rush hour in the Metro and see how it feels!

Just as there are many needy people in this world (more than half the world's population, at last count), so too is there much philanthropy. I cannot help but notice, though, that even the most generous among us usually like to broadcast their giving. I have heard and seen the names of donors announced and published not only in magazines, newspapers, and online, but even in some temples in Asia! That makes me cringe. True giving is unconditional, free of ego and without expectation of return. It is without any hidden or overt agenda. Such giving can be a deeply joyful and memorable experience. In fact, in real giving, the giver may not even remember to whom he gave, or what he gave, so there is no question of expecting anything in return. Pure giving is an automatic spiritual action, but the moment we bring in the "I" and the "I gave such a beautiful _____," it becomes an egoistic action and loses its value at the spiritual level.

Let us now broaden our concept of giving. Meaningful giving can also include intangible gifts, such as guidance, love, and affection in relationships. Among the more obvious examples is the way that most parents generously give these to their children. But human nature works in strange ways. When such giving involves feelings of fear or expectation, the spirit behind it can become clouded, or contaminated. I can think of an example of this in my own life. As a schoolteacher, I used to counsel my students, guide them to improve their performance, and support them with sincerity in whatever way I could. I was very patient with them, and it seemed to work quite well. Then one day, I began to question why I could not handle my own children in the same way. Why couldn't I give to my own kin what I was giving so effectively to other children?

The answer came to me as an important revelation. I was afraid that in the failure of my children, I would see my own failure as a parent. There was an expectation lurking behind the love and guidance I was giving them—I did not want to fail. Often I would find myself taking out my frustration on them because of my fear of failure. My ego was putting pressure on me and I was passing this along, consciously and unconsciously, to my children, making matters worse. I realized that I was very subjective with them because I loved them dearly. This was in fact preventing me from giving effective guidance and support to them. The added ego pressure was very subtle, yet powerful in the effect it had on our relationship.

However, one day, after my awakening, I suddenly understood what unconditional giving in relationships actually means. Breaking the cycle, I distanced myself from my ego trips and became more detached, yet sincere, in handling my children. This called for rigorous practice, and in the beginning I had to pause, become aware of my feelings, and pass bravely through the energy of my fears. Gradually, however, I was able to find ways of dealing with them in a refreshingly ego—free way. I deliberately kept my egoistic expectations and the prospects of failure out of my mind. No longer was I parenting them in the earlier tension mode, and they could feel the change. My message to them was a clear one, of accepting them unconditionally. My love and guidance were unconditional constants.

This change in my behavior brought a remarkable change in them, and in our relationship. The transformation happened very discreetly and gradually. Our communication not only improved, but also became very healthy and supportive. In unconditional giving, I received what anybody would want—the grace of a harmonious and loving relationship.

I've since come to see that expectations in any relationship are desperate bids to fill the dreaded inner void that seems to reside within us, making us feel incomplete. Expectations come from a desire to feel loved, wanted, valuable, and worthy of attention. All of these express some aspect of the ego's insecurity and lack of self-esteem. Without understanding and addressing this root cause, trying to fill up that void externally with a return of gift or favor, cannot get us very far. We might equate such attention and gifts with love, and tell ourselves that the more stuff and praise we get, the more we are loved. But in reality, that would only serve to make such expectations unending, and ensure that the void—now a bottomless pit—would never be filled.

But even after I identified the limitations and potential damage caused by ego-driven "giving" in relationships, the practical application of this principle was still a challenge. A natural extension of this principle was that I not expect anything in return from colleagues, siblings, and friends. This proved arduous, but gave me freedom.

As I moved in this direction, I started deliberately ignoring many things in my interactions with my wider family groups and friends: the "do's and don'ts," the "should" and "should not," the "have to" and "don't have to" in terms of behavior and expectations. If I felt like talking to some friends and family, I called them; if I felt like giving something; I gave, without expecting the other person to reciprocate in time, energy, or gifts. If I did not get any response, it did not bother me at all. I felt liberated! When we feel liberated in this way, we free the other person as well, from blame and guilt for not reaching up to our expectations.

Removing expectations from our thinking eradicates (or at least reduces) the feeling of blame. There is then no room for the other person to feel guilty for what would ordinarily have been "expected" but was not done. We are not cornering anybody, or making anyone feel that he has committed a crime or hurtful faux pas by not fulfilling our expectations. This attitude, this space-giving, precludes a situation in which "the other" has to keep on proving, justifying, and explaining why he could not do what should have been done. Most important, we do not pass judgment. We do not drain energy from our relationships— and they thrive!

When I look around, I see a lot of relationships that are selfish and egoistic. People do things for others, but generally with the hope or expectation of getting commensurate "payback" at some future point. They "keep score." In Asia, some people even bring up children with the unspoken expectation that they will be looked after by them in old age. This may be the cultural norm, and simply accepted according to the customary way of doing things. But I have often felt that this kind of love can be suffocating and stifling, as it produces feelings of guilt and blame when it is not reciprocated. It is egoistic, and the energy that flows in this kind of love is heavy and dense, which is not in anybody's interest.

On the other hand, any relationship will thrive when we focus on what we can give and not on what we can get. In a subtle way, such an exchange of love becomes more enduring. This is because the enlivening energy that flows through such relationships is very pure and clear.

This is an important lesson, as all relationships work better when there is an "equal" exchange of energy. When a relationship drains someone, for whatever reason, there is an imbalance of energy. And this can only lead to a chain of power games. When manipulation and one-upmanship rear their ugly heads, people play external games to gain external power and feel internally complete. Thus is attention diverted from the real cause of the void that exists within us.

The same applies to any loving relationship. Unconditional love in any relationship is energy that flows without any strings attached. It is light and flexible and supportive between the people concerned. The receiver feels the vibrations of unconditional love and experiences the freedom that comes with such love. This freedom lightens and elevates the energies, as the relationship becomes more loving. Love given in this spacious milieu is spiritually uplifting, as it does not carry any negative emotions. The exchange of loving energy happens at a very discreet level. Only the giver and the receiver can sense its vibrations. They are then able and eager to pass on this love to others, thereby creating an atmosphere of kindness and compassion.

My Reflections

....
....
....
....
....
....
....
....
....
....
....
....
....
....
....
....
....
....

5
Love thy pain

"To accept something is not to agree with it. It is simply to embrace it, whether you agree with it or not. You give something your blessings when you give it your best energies, your highest thoughts."

Neale Donald Walsch

Some years back, my mother had a knee replacement surgery done, after agonizing over the decision for several years. As you can imagine, it was a painful procedure. For the first few days after surgery she was in deep pain. She couldn't move, couldn't turn around, and was totally dependent on others for her personal needs. This frustrated her and made her angry with everyone. However, after a few months she apparently forgot about all the agony and annoyance, and was ready to get a similar procedure for her second knee.

That left me puzzled. How could this happen? After being in so much pain from the first surgery, how did she find the drive so soon for the next one? Similarly, why is it that after suffering intense pain during childbirth, many women are eager to have another child the very next year?

Our memory of physical pain can be short-lived. We can forget or file it away as soon as our body is back to normal. Some consider such selective memory loss a gift! If human memory is so short-lived, then why is it that we hold on to our painful emotions and resentments for years and years? If our memory is so fleeting or sketchy when it comes to physical pain, then the same logic should apply to our emotional pain as well. But we know that does not happen.

When a dog bites us, we seek immediate medical attention and go along with it; we accept the event and get ourselves treated without any resentment. We move on with our lives. Then why can't we do the same thing when *people* hurt us? In life, we come across a variety of people, all with unique predispositions and interests. There will inevitably be strong disagreements with some and we may suffer hurt from others. When people hurt us, many of us remember each and every incident, every subtle slight, every word uttered, and even the intonation that was used. But why do we hold on to the negative feelings when people cause us pain, when all this really achieves is prolong our own suffering? If we can forgive a dog, then why can't we forgive our fellow human beings who, presumably like the dog, "know not what they do"?

Clearly, for physical hurt and its cure, we *accept* the situation, whereas when people hurt us we resent it. And it is this ironclad grip on resentment that changes our pain into suffering. It is the constriction of resentment and non-acceptance of a situation that "turns the screws," making us feel the pain more, as we internalize it, personalize it, and get angry about it. We then look for ways to take revenge, overtly or more often subtly, by somehow hurting others or ourselves, which itself brings more pain. And so the cycle goes on!

We meet many different kinds of people in life, some with whom we have pleasant interactions, and others with whom we do not. Or at least, that's the view from the physical plane. From a spiritual perspective, each person has come into our life either to teach us something, or to learn some lessons from us. In Hindu scriptures, this concept has been further elaborated as the Law of Karma. People participate in our lives to clear some of their past karma through us, or to help us resolve some of our own through them. But we choose to remain unaware of this deeper purpose.

For many of us, this can be a tough pill to swallow. All of us, at some point or another in our lives, have encountered relationships and experiences that have caused us pain. It can be instructive to reflect on the purpose of these experiences beyond the physical level, pausing to ask ourselves why we have encountered them. If we simply resent them, or the very presence of those who have hurt us, we also reject the spiritual teaching that they offer, which is a truly priceless gift to us from the Universe. We thus lose an opportunity to grow spiritually.

The dynamics of this spiritual learning are such that we are sure to encounter different people who will teach us the same lesson through similar kinds of experiences. The particulars of these learning experiences may well vary, but the underlying intent will be the same. Here we see the Law of Attraction expressing in an instructive way. An angry person will attract the experience of more angry people in his life; a jealous person will attract people and experiences that expose this negative emotion within him. This helps bring our negative emotions into the light of day, as only in this awareness can we realize that we need to do something about it. And so it continues, until we finally learn our real lessons and "remember" our true nature, which is that of a kind and compassionate person who is full of love.

So when you repeatedly encounter people of a disagreeable nature in your life—say, people who all exhibit a similar attribute like anger, jealousy, and dishonesty—understand that this is because at a spiritual level, you are attracting the same kind of *lesson* that needs to be learnt. Perhaps some people will teach you to be more compassionate or more forgiving and loving. Or it is upon you to teach them!

Spiritual learning starts the instant we become aware of our negative emotions, and is realized when they dissolve in love and faith in the True Source.

It is only when I became aware of this Truth that I was able to stop resenting unpleasant experiences in my past and understand the real reason for going through them. I understood how those experiences had made me a better person. They helped me to understand the qualities I had ingrained in my character because of them. At that moment I had tears of joy in my eyes! I mentally thanked the very same people for helping me to grow. It is at that moment that I began to love the pain I had felt earlier. I had finally learned to forgive.

My Reflections

6

Insecurities and self – esteem

"When you lose touch with inner stillness, you lose touch with yourself. When you lose touch with yourself, you lose yourself in the world. Your innermost sense of self, of who you are, is inseparable from stillness. This is the I AM that is deeper than name and form."

Eckhart Tolle

Most of us live with insecurities of one kind or another, though we may not be aware that they are lurking inside us. I have often wondered, are these of our innate nature, or do we develop them along the way? It is important to become aware and tuned in about this, as insecurity has a bearing on our spiritual growth.

Why do we feel insecure so often, even when we have so many things to be thankful for in our life? A successful and rich person is often insecure about losing his wealth; a poor person is insecure about feeding his family. Beyond these physical concerns, there are insecurities about losing love, losing appreciation at work, losing physical beauty, and so on.

Sometimes we can see traces of insecurity even in a three-year-old child, who tries to keep his toys to himself while playing with friends. A child can get jealous when a parent shows affection or special admiration for a sibling. I do not believe that we are born with such insecurity. But at some point during our childhood, this sense of insecurity appears, and I suspect that for most people it only gets stronger as they go through their life. The tragedy is that such insecurities lead to low self-esteem. We then somehow start building our shaky self-esteem on what others say and do. Our sense of self and our identity become almost totally dependent on what others think of us.

Parents have a particularly strong impact on the development of self-esteem in their children from a very early age. Psychological and emotional problems are known to arise in children who do not grow with enough self-esteem. When parents regard their children as *kids*, underlings who must follow their direction because parents are in command, they diminish their self-esteem. On the contrary, when we treat them as "little people," listening to them, showing unconditional love, explaining without criticizing, they feel secure and grounded within. Self-esteem flourishes.

Our duty as parents becomes even more important in light of how these internal insecurities affect the spiritual growth of our children. Parents and family members must be ever mindful of how and what is said to them. Negative comments made even jokingly to children can erode their self-esteem. And this can only reinforce their inclination to continuously look outside of themselves for inner peace and comfort.

Often unknowingly, we attempt to build our self-esteem upon external factors. We try to find our grounding in our education, our job, our social status, our wealth, our knowledge, our strength, and our looks— anything that seems to give us or demonstrate power over others.

This can become like a bottomless pit—the more one puts in, the more it needs to be filled. We find our solace in external power, which makes us feel good and strong. But the better we feel about our job or our looks, and the more compliments we get, the more praise we crave. Such "feedback" can make us increasingly dependent upon "them" (and what "they" say) to feel good about ourselves. A fashion model likes to be praised for her looks and poise, and identifies herself with her beauty; a scholarly person is commended for his wealth of ideas and "finds himself" in academia. We get caught in forever chasing these "externals," sometimes over the course of a lifetime. Many believe that enhancing their faux identities is the purpose of their life. But ask any rich person if he is "in joy," and you may be told how many sleepless nights or discordant relationships he has suffered, despite his wealth. Ask a highly qualified person with a good job, and he is likely to mention worry over bills, or being overextended, or fears over a career rat race.

We find ourselves scrambling to fill the void, an emptiness that deepens in us from childhood and builds false ideas and beliefs about ourselves. Spurred on by these insecurities, we feel incomplete, and aspire to happiness. Some people shop to feel complete within, momentarily filling the void with cartloads of perishables. Others stuff their faces with "goodies." But after a short while, they are back to where they started. If happiness were in objects, all of us would derive the same degree of happiness from the same objects for all time to come. But by the very nature of material things, the pleasure they give is short-lived. Running after temporary objects is naturally going to give us only temporary happiness.

After my awakening, I understood that our *true and enduring* security and self-esteem come only as we move closer to our True Source. We need to draw on this one reality, rather than on short-lived external factors, to be strengthened internally. As we grow spiritually, we become aware of the difference between enjoyment and being in a state of joy. Material objects lose their appeal. We are no longer dependent upon others to make us feel "complete." As our connection to the Divine becomes increasingly apparent, we begin to grow in our inner world.

My Reflections

....

....

....

....

....

....

....

....

....

....

....

....

....

....

....

....

....

....

Part Two

EGO

Our Very Own, Loud and Proud

7
The unrelenting grip of ego

"Give up all bad habits in you, banish the ego and develop the spirit of surrender. You will then experience bliss."

Sri Sathya Sai Baba

Among the various stumbling blocks in spiritual development, the most difficult one is the individual ego. And this is something most of us have in great abundance!

At a very basic and commonly understood level, ego can be equated with pride, arrogance, vanity, or self-absorption. It may operate subtly, but very often quite powerfully and conspicuously. It profoundly impacts the way we live, interact with others, and grow spiritually. Let us discuss some aspects of this influence in the next few essays.

We have all seen manifestations of ego in successful people around us. When they are living their material dream, and everything in life is working according to plan, there is sometimes a particular aura in their personality, an arrogance and grandiosity accompanying the belief that they are entitled to everything in their lives. You can see this in their demeanor and hear it in their conversations. In addition to boasting, subtly or not so subtly, about what they have achieved and what they possess, their discussions focus mainly or entirely on themselves. It is as if they are in a constant monologue on their favorite theme.

Another quality that one might see in such people is their apparent compulsion to disclose the price of the things they buy. There is an element of vanity clearly visible. They talk about their "connections" to higher-ups and people in cool or powerful positions, name-dropping at every opportunity. Humility and modesty are conspicuously absent—qualities that they themselves may not even notice in others or consider them as a weakness.

It seems that this trait represents a problem of attribution and a lack of gratitude. Their ego has encouraged them to attribute all of their success to their own effort. They may also see it as an inevitable companion to their highborn status! The way they see it, no one else played much role in their good fortune. Consequently, they do not even recognize the support they have surely received from the Universe, and have little or no feeling of gratitude. In reality, their inner connection to the Divine is as yet weak. Their power and feeling of completeness still depend entirely on the outer trappings of success.

Compare this individual to a person who is down on his luck, one who has lost everything—money, family, work, and so on. Such a person lacks all the sources of external power that we earlier associated with the manifestation of ego. He is without all supports and protective layers and covers, which might have earlier given him feelings of superiority over others, or just simple adequacy. Logically, one might expect this person to be ego-free.

But no, the dynamics of ego are interesting! Ego hangs in there, not budging from the person who has little nourishment to offer it. It just changes its shape.

The "outcast's" reconfigured ego often manifests as denial, non-acceptance of the situation, and a superficial attempt to control others through negative means. Stealing, lying, and a dazzling array of other vices are often resorted to when a person attempts to regain lost external power. Abuse of people who are weaker than him—including women and children—may also give the feeling of power. The more others suffer at his hands, the more twisted satisfaction he derives, as harming others replenishes his stock of external power. All attempts to manipulate others by intimidating or humiliating them are deployed to regain and reclaim lost power. Temporarily, of course!

A person who has lost all external power tries to get it back by blaming others for his situation. He plays a total blame game—blaming God for his situation, blaming his parents for having given him birth, criticizing everyone for not doing enough to rescue him, not trusting anyone, and believing that everyone is trying to take advantage of him. Blaming others absolves him of not taking responsibility for his actions, or accepting their consequences. He finds it difficult to accept his mistakes, as that would require introspection, acknowledgement of misjudgment and misdeeds, and the humble awareness of what he needs to learn. And that would mean an acceptance of defeat, and hence a loss of ego. He may also indulge in addictions as a remedy, which we shall discuss later. This is the typical mindscape and behavior of a person who has lost power, both externally and internally.

I recall the case of a neighbor some years back. He was highly educated and had a career with a promising future. He knew this, and yet did not deign to accept average jobs, even when he was unemployed. They were beneath his dignity, he would say. As a result, he never held a steady job that could support him and his family. Finally he ended up perpetually unemployed and living on financial support from his sibling. And the amazing thing was that instead of being grateful for this support, he frequently jealously complained about the quality of his sibling's life, as he himself could not live in the same way. Again, we see the unrelenting distortions of ego at play.

My shift toward spirituality opened me up to becoming aware of ego in all its hydra-headed expressions. I began to notice when it is active or inactive, when it is dormant, and how it springs up again and again in my interactions with people. I notice this so clearly now in people I meet and, truth be told, in my own behavior as well.

I believe that only through this awareness and constant vigilance can we begin to deny ego its joyless joyride and move forward toward spiritual living.

My Reflections

....

....

....

....

....

....

....

....

....

....

....

....

....

....

....

....

....

....

....

8

Ego in relationships

"You need your ego to survive in the three-dimensional world, but you need only that part of the ego which processes information. The rest—pride, arrogance, defensiveness, fear—is worse than useless. The rest of the ego separates you from wisdom, joy, and God."

Brian Weiss

The presence of ego in human psyche never ceases to amaze me for its unrelenting ability to blind us to the Divine. Let us now see how it disturbs loving relationships.

In order to satisfy the needs of our ego, we often indulge in external power games. By external power I mean forces outside ourselves that give us a feeling of superiority over others and make us feel stronger and complete inside, usually at the expense of others.

We don't realize how much of our time and energy is wasted looking for ways to experience such external power. How much time is lost in thinking and manipulating to make other people do what we want? Think of a boss who habitually shouts at his subordinates, thus creating an unpleasant atmosphere within the workplace. Whatever impact his behavior may have on the feelings of subordinates, the boss relishes the feeling of power that he gets as a result.

Observe people who adamantly hold on to their opinions during a group discussion. I often hear such people speaking very forcibly, sometimes in an intimidating or tauntingly interrogative tone of voice. Their ego is too strong to give in and accept that their interlocutor could also have a point and be right in his own way. When I see people arguing very aggressively in this manner, I mentally cringe. Why have we forgotten to discuss civilly? Is there not an ego-free way for us to agree to disagree?

At times, I see an argument between two people that starts on one topic and progresses to another; by the end of two hours of fruitless volleying, the point on which they had begun their discussion is lost. To me, this suggests that their main goal right along was to *win an argument* and *prove themselves right, and the other person wrong.* In this attempt to establish their "rightness," they may seize upon unrelated and lateral topics, propelled by fears of failure and dreams of "glory." There is never a conclusion—or even points of agreement—to the topic of discussion. What could have been a lively and thought-provoking exchange becomes a titanic clash of *egos.* Needless to say, there is neither an opening nor closure to the topic at hand.

I also see this pattern all too often among parents and children. Parents tend to assume that because they are older, they are always right. When my kids were young, I was guilty of this too. The truth is that biological age does not always confer wisdom, though it may often grant a larger and more devious ego!

When we play power games, much thinking and preparation is required before we can actually win an argument forcibly. Our body movement, our facial expressions, and our composure are all unnaturally "off." Our heartbeat and the knots in our stomach are clear giveaways of the fears and anxieties with which our mind is occupied. How much effort did we have to put in to feign absolute rightness and superiority, while also making this charade look as natural as possible? Compare this to a discussion in which we are a compassionate listener and open to another's point of view. The mind is totally relaxed and at peace, because when we are compassionate and free of ego, we speak from the heart; we speak the language of the soul.

When two egos clash, the repercussions are not just momentary and local, but can be harmful to the relationship itself. Reverberating in the atmosphere of the house or workplace, they may also raise troubling doubts about love and trust between people and, in worse cases, threaten the relationship. Fears and suspicions may arise subconsciously, even if not articulated. This proliferation of ugly possibilities leads inevitably to a series of new arguments, which leave one or the other member having to prove and explain what he or she meant, versus what was understood. At this point, a box of "Band-Aids" may be whipped out to "patch up" the situation. These temporary fixes may come in the form of a tactical "retreat," or a polite but empty "sorry," meant to maintain peace and move on. In fact, when apologies are made to "keep the peace," they are also made at the ego level, as a favor to the other person. This is because the ego has not really disengaged from the situation. It is still there, festering inside, ready to spring up and bite at the next opportunity.

As long as there is one-upmanship and a strong undercurrent of ego in relationships, we are building temporary relationships, built on sand. No relationship can thrive when the ego runs so strong. It is bad enough when two family members are egoistic, but when everyone in the family operates in the same way, the results are predictable—disastrous.

One ego needs another ego to play against and thrive. That is the essence of power games. But this equation loses its power when neutralized by a spiritually aware and connected person. That is why if one person is not egoistic in a family, he has the ability to reduce the ego-driven traits of the other family members, and bring them closer to Truth. Take away ego completely, or significantly diminish it in any relationship, and you will see both sides blossoming into their potential. Then, the relationship becomes mutually supportive and the results can be astounding. I call this the very benign ripple effect when an ego is dissolving.

Like oil and water, ego and spirituality do not mix. When a person keeps all his attention on I, me, my, and mine, the connection to his true Self, the *inner* Self, feels detached. Prayers and meditation in such cases would be of little value. Humility, I feel, is the foremost quality for spiritual growth. It brings gratitude into our hearts, which automatically subdues our ego. It helps one to recognize the omnipresent hand of the

Divine in all that we do. It inspires our hearts to look away from the distraction of temporary external power, and activates that ever-so-subtle Source of true internal power.

Of course, this does not happen in a day or two, and it could take even years or lifetimes for the ego to dissolve. Awareness is just the first step!

My Reflections

....
....
....
....
....
....
....
....
....
....
....
....
....
....
....
....
....
....
....
....
....

9

In control or out of control?

"Not all thinking and all emotion are of the ego. They turn into ego only when you identify with them and they take you over completely, that is to say, when they become "I."

Eckhart Tolle

If you look objectively at relationships, you'll notice that some people get very obsessed about controlling others. Controlling others is a common way of gaining external power. Spiritually speaking, though, are the controllers not out of control themselves?

I know a bustling urban household in Wellington, New Zealand that offers an interesting insight of a family where the housewife is truly the ultimate control freak. Her husband, a successful business executive, and two teenage children have no say in what they wear, what they do, and where they go. She decides these matters. She needs to know their whereabouts at all times of the day. It seems to me that she even wants to control how they breathe!

When her daughter left home to attend University in Auckland, her mother took it upon herself to phone her every morning so that she would not be late for class; she was not allowed to go out late at night without Mom's permission. His mother had to know what she was eating and how she was dressing and so on. I often wondered, did this kind of control come from concern about her daughter? Or was her "worry" more about losing control over her daughter?

I have seen similar behavior patterns in other families as well, with one or the other spouse playing this dominant role. These control freaks must have their house set up exactly the way *they* want. They just cannot handle it if other family members do what they need to do, or disrupt their very precise arrangements and routines in any way. No one in the family is allowed to move things around, as that would upset their feeling of control and their sense of permanence and balance.

I feel that this kind of behavior arises when a person's sense of identity depends entirely upon how much of his/her immediate surroundings he/she can control. People whose self-esteem is low need to get external power by controlling members of their own family or inner circle. They need to feel in command over others to feel good about themselves. This satisfies their ego and makes them feel complete. If others do not follow their dictates, they step up their power games to get their way. These maneuvers could include interrogative or intimidating styles of control; they could morph into the dejected "poor me" persona, or the ever popular "silent treatment"—whatever it takes to get others to bend to their will.

Often, the sequence does not quite end there. The "controlled" also need to correct their balance, and will look for other ways of gaining external power and refilling themselves to satisfy their ego. And so the cycle goes on!

Does this sound familiar?

From a spiritual perspective, such behavior is actually quite fascinating. Let us dig a little deeper. Ego takes various "shapes" and comes in a variety of colors. We often see a child sulking in a corner for flimsy reasons, as children are wont to do. Parents like to call these childish tantrums, but there are really children reaching out for external power, learning the levers of control. Sometimes I see elderly people frequently complain about just about everything around them. This behavior pattern is also to seek attention that they have lost and miss. They are actually in dire need of "power." They are poster children of the Poor-Me Syndrome. The question then is, how should we address the early signs of this pattern that we see in a child, so that it does not remain with a person through the adult life?

At the workplace, a boss who uses his position to gratuitously flaunt his authority is also looking for external power. I am told that some corporations encourage a culture in which "stripes" of authority are openly displayed. Contrast this with those who reach high positions of authority as leaders and yet have no need to constantly remind those around them of their position. They feel internally complete, perhaps, and know that they do not have to worry about losing anything.

If you look around, you may see similar patterns of manifestation of ego. A person who constantly judges others and belittles them as a matter of course; a person who shows off his possessions; a person who has a habit of blaming others, rightly or wrongly; a person who quietly enjoys making people feel uncomfortable and guilty. These are people who, lacking a true sense of themselves, also have little internal power. To feel good about themselves, they need to dominate and control others, always in charge of everything and everybody.

What they don't know is that this sort of control actually does not serve their purpose well. It satisfies their ego only temporarily. Based on lies, it must reestablish itself again and again. That's why the pattern is so hard to break. Only when the dominator becomes aware that his seeming gain is temporary and not meaningful at all, does real internal power begin to be felt.

Welcoming their connection to the Divine Source is the only way they, or anyone, can feel complete. A spiritual person does not need to control others. His self-esteem and internal power come not from imposing his will, but from connection with the Divine Source. That is where his spiritual nourishment comes from. This nourishment is unlimited. Its presence brings internal calm, and can be harmoniously projected outward, into the relationships that he tried to control earlier.

This awareness is prerequisite to ego-free relationships.

My Reflections

10
Drainer or "drainee?"

"If you want to reach a state of bliss, then go beyond your ego and the internal dialogue. Make a decision to relinquish the need to control, the need to be approved, and the need to judge. Those are the three things the ego is doing all the time."

Deepak Chopra

When I look around among the people I know or have met, from the perspective of energy I can often observe two extreme kinds of people— those whom I call the drainers and the others the "drainees."

Drainers are those who regularly find ways to drain energy from others in order to feed their external power needs and to feel complete. They are popularly known as "psychic vampires." They constantly demand that people in their life make them feel happy and complete. But whatever they receive in terms of time, energy, and support is never enough. You give them time, and they also need moral support; you give them moral support, and they expect something else, perhaps financial support. They have a laundry list of expectations and needs, and are ever-extracting goods, services, and miscellaneous "support" from the likeliest targets.

They are often appreciative when others are good to them. Yet, they usually proceed to judge with a critical eye to see what else might be done. They are likely to be searching for a selfish motive behind every kind gesture. Since drainers are almost always judgmental and are, in a way, testing others' love for them, they make people feel guilty for not always living up to their lofty expectations. They will not miss an opportunity to blame others for falling short of their "duties" toward them. There is just no pleasing them.

They are generally unable to reciprocate with the love and attention that others need from them. Their own demands are so high that others are sometimes hesitant to ask them for attention or help. They are like the bottomless pit we gaped into earlier. The more that gets put in, the more its insatiable appetite calls for *more*. At the same time, they are always looking for others to validate their needs, beliefs, opinions and behavior. That makes them feel that they are *right*. The root issue of course is that, unaware of their true being in Divine Source, their internal power is inherently weak.

On the other hand, "drainees" are the ones who continue to give unconditionally. Sometimes "drainees" themselves have a malaise called "disease to please." They just cannot say *no* to a request, as not only are they genuinely kind, but they do not want to be in anybody's bad graces. They are willing to continuously give off their time and energy to demands that may sometimes be unreasonable, not wanting to hurt or disappoint others. This trait also indicates weak internal power, as it demonstrates their craving for acceptance. Taken to an even greater extreme, there are those who become such habitual "givers" that they either simply forget what they themselves need, or feel that they do not deserve anything good for themselves. They are willing to give the best of their things and their efforts, as they feel they do not deserve them. They may also delude themselves into believing that being a human "Giving Tree," stripped of its leaves, boughs, and bark, makes them somehow holy, or nobly superior. This trait too reflects weak internal power.

There is an interesting phenomenon associated with "drainees." Some of them keep giving willingly, and appear to be happy to "fill" their vampiric followers. Giving comes naturally to them, and they do not even remember what they gave and to whom. These are the unconditional givers. Others, however, also do their best to fill those bottomless pits, willingly or unwillingly, but then find themselves resenting it. This is a big problem, for herein lies the source of much emotional baggage. Whether conscious or unconscious, their resentment can only lead to anger and frustration, as they find it difficult to carry on in such a drained and angry state. They feel empty inside. They are like volcanoes waiting to erupt.

The spiritual correlate of the drainer-drainee equation is that the Universe functions in a way by which the flow of love is eventually balanced. Love is, after all, energy, and energy that is being drained excessively and not returned has to find its equilibrium somehow. I feel that this principle is sometimes demonstrated within the lifetime of an affected individual, and even beyond.

I can share the example of my own grandfather. He was a medical service provider in rural India who looked after people, cared for them, and was a generous giver all through his adult life and into old age. Before he passed away, at the age of 90, he went through two years in a coma. I often wondered why he faced this tragic end after living such a generous life. I can now rationalize it from a clear perspective. He had given to people for years and years, and so before he passed away, perhaps that was his soul's way of getting back and receiving the same kind of love and care that he had showered on others.

A spiritually inclined person is neither a drainer nor a drainee. He respects himself—his time, his energy—and would not drain anybody; nor would he give in to the unreasonable demands of drainers. He maintains this fine energy balance internally, at all times. His self-esteem and his humility both come from connection with the Divine Source. He feels thoroughly and perpetually complete.

My Reflections

11

Ego's play in addictions

"People spend a lifetime searching for happiness; looking for peace. They chase idle dreams, addictions, religions, even other people, hoping to fill the emptiness that plagues them. The irony is the only place they ever needed to search was within."

Ramona L. Anderson

Have you considered why people are addicted to substances or certain kinds of behavior? What really happens when a person regularly hits the bottle or indulges obsessively in gambling, sex, or drugs? Can spirituality play a role in helping deal with addictions?

I recall a young middle class family in our neighborhood when I lived in India many years ago. I was very young at that time and I remember seeing him as a family man, with a lovely wife and three wonderful children I often played with. Then one day we were shocked to learn of how his entire life had collapsed around him. He had become an alcoholic, we learnt. When the urge to indulge in the addiction came, nothing was more important to him. He eventually lost everything— his relationships, his family, and his job. I didn't quite know what issues led him to this addiction, but felt saddened and puzzled by this turn of events nevertheless.

There are, of course, ever so many other families that have similarly faced emotional and financial ruin due to some kind of addiction of a family member.

On the surface, an addiction is the behavior that results from an extreme absence of external and internal power. Indulgence in the addiction gives the victim a temporary sense of power or escape—the power and "rush" of easy money from gambling, or the seeming escape in buying sex, or temporarily diverting the mind with drugs. An addiction may start when the person loses external power in any area—professional, personal, financial—and is groping for something to fill up the vacuum. Or it could be an unacknowledged habit that "crept up" and turned into an addiction that has thrown the person out of control. The dynamics of addictions are such that once they take hold of a person's mind, they exert greater force than can be countered by normal self-control. Like a magnet, addiction pulls one inexorably toward some desperately sought relief, and the person becomes a slave to the addiction.

At the deepest level, there is often searing emotional pain behind addictions—fears that the person does not want to accept, and cannot or will not deal with. Addictions give him a place where he can hide from his painful emotions. No amount of explanation and advice helps when an addiction has overtaken the mind and body completely. The reason is that when we try to explain consequences to an addict, he may be in such confusion and denial that he cannot respond to the logic. Explanations reach the mind but not the painful feelings and emotions. That is why counseling may provide only temporary relief.

At a subtler level, addictions are basically negative energy vibrations. Negative vibrations will, of course, attract negative vibrations of a similar frequency, so that one addiction may lead to another. It is for this reason that addicted people often get sucked into a range of other vices, which only make matters worse. This hastens and exacerbates the decline, as the person is caught in the cycle of satisfying his addiction, experiencing temporary power, loss of power, and the mad scramble for another "fix."

As mentioned earlier, when there is nothing left to base his self-esteem upon, he blames other people or his god for his situation. This blame game is easy, as it absolves him of his responsibilities. The irony is that when one is feeling down in life, out of control and without external power, he blames the *one* source of recovery that would work—faith in the helping hand of the Universe. He tends to block out that potential ally, the only source of wisdom and strength that could connect him to his internal power and make him feel complete.

A spiritual connection leaves no place for nervous breakdowns, addictions, or depression. It makes external power irrelevant. It leads us along a different path and gives us an unlimited source of internal power by which our self-esteem is maintained and felt as a connection with the Divine. It gives us different coping strategies that are not ego-based, but rather faith-based and wholly beneficent. It does not then matter if mistakes have been made in the past. There is no place for self-blame or guilt on a beautifully "clean slate." All that matters is the vast reservoir of love that this Source provides, which can be the true and most effective remedy for any addiction. That is the power of faith in the Divine Source.

My Reflections

....

....

....

....

....

....

....

....

....

....

....

....

....

....

....

....

....

....

....

....

12

Mirror, mirror, on the wall...

"Abundance is not something we acquire. It is something we tune into."

Wayne Dyer

We have looked at some aspects of ego and how it affects relationships and stunts our spiritual growth. Another consequence of ego is how it distorts our relationship with the Universe.

We have earlier discussed people who appear to have everything, who could be considered rich by any normal standards. Their identity too often comes from the material objects they possess in abundance. Yet, it is interesting to see that in spite of all that they possess, many feel that they do not have enough. Nothing is enough! They could have the best of everything and yet still not see or feel the abundance; they feel only insufficiency.

Of course, the word "best" is entirely subjective and relative. My concept of 'best' will surely be different from somebody else's. Yet why would those who possess all they have ever aspired to, want *more*?

Such malcontents do not value the abundance that the Divine Source has bestowed on them, and see only lack. Their behavior and language do not reflect gratitude or joyous acknowledgement of what they have.

On the contrary, they tend to "compare and contrast," ever looking at those who have more. Comparing their material possessions with those on the next rung up, they find that they do not have enough. They may talk about their destiny or bad luck, and how unfortunate they are when they cannot buy one more exorbitant bauble, or experience one more personal accolade. The fact is that they will always find someone who has more. Not being grateful for what we have, and comparing ourselves with others, is surely a recipe for frustration, anger, and blame.

Such people can be awash in loving friends and family members, and yet feel very lonely inside. Unable to value what their family does for them, they are always on the lookout for things that the family did *not* do. They find it difficult to relate to others, as they project faults onto everyone, actively seeking the negative in them. Nobody does enough for them. There is a nagging feeling of deprivation in virtually all of their interactions with people.

We can understand such thinking and feeling in people who are poor, who lack food, clothing, shelter, and basic necessities. But what can we say to those who have been blessed with everything, and are still feeling deprived?

When they look at themselves in the mirror, despite their wealth, they will see themselves as the "poorest." Somehow, they do not seem able to receive the love and warmth that comes their way. The more they get, the more they feel deprived, or even wronged—they surely are the poorest among all.

As mentioned earlier, this delusion of lack is continuously expressed, not only in their thoughts but also in their words and actions. Such people are continuously broadcasting messages of neediness and despair to the Universe, and the Universe responds in kind, validating what they think. Thus negatively "affirmed" and reinforced, the attraction of more and more unhappy experiences is sure to follow. For this reason, deep inside they always feel lonely, incomplete, and miserable.

There is yet another dimension to this feeling of deprivation. It's a dimension that some of us don't even notice in the way we perceive our lives and the world around us. We often see the proverbial glass as being half-empty, oblivious to or only fleetingly aware of what life has blessed us with. We take so very much for granted in our lives! I have visited slums in Mumbai and Jakarta, and I will never forget the look in the eyes of the sick and undernourished children there. Such haunting memories always remind me of the blessings that I have in my life.

If we reflect on our lives, we will find much to rejoice about. For starters, most of us are lucky to have been born with our physical and mental faculties working correctly. We don't control any of this, and take the elegantly efficient functioning of our body for granted. The human body is an amazing miracle in every way! We're all quick to applaud the inventors of computers and software, but what about the creator of this efficient and self-repairing machine we call our body?

Is it conceivable that this seemingly unconscious disregard is precisely because we have allowed our blessings, our full glass, to strengthen our ego, rather than strengthen our gratitude?

It seems we have blinded ourselves to what the Universe offers us unconditionally. The Universe does not ask us to give anything in return for its life-giving energy from the Sun. It does not charge us for or ration the air that we breathe and the water that we drink. Yet we still find reasons to complain when things—even the weather—do not work according to our wishes and expectations.

When one has known the touch of connection with the Divine, one feels "rich" from within. One sees abundance and beauty everywhere he looks and breathes, as the heart brims over in love and joy. To gain abundance, we need to *feel* that we are living in abundance. We need to be grateful to the Divine for all its blessings. In gratitude, we attract more blessings. The Universe responds to our deepest thoughts. That is the Law of Attraction. And just by changing our thoughts and feelings, we can change the way we experience life.

My Reflections

Part Three

EMOTIONAL BLOCKAGES

The Silent but Violent Sting

13

Beauty, brains, or the heart?

"The human heart feels things the eyes cannot see and knows what the mind cannot understand."

Robert Valett

It is our nature to continuously search for our identity, mistakenly believed to be a constellation of habits, beliefs and circumstances that define us and make us feel complete inside. We instinctively feel the need for it. Yet, for many of us, this quest can take an entire lifetime, simply because we do not know where to look!

As we have discussed earlier, our lives often remain focused on external power and its trappings. When we enjoy this power, it becomes an end in itself. External power in our personalities is validated by others around us, and needs this ongoing validation to survive. When others compliment and praise us, they "reaffirm" our existence emotionally, and fortify our self-esteem. That is why so many of us hoard things, and cling to people who give us this power. Despite the ups and downs, emotional swings, and the damage to relationships occasioned by our craving and clinging, we generally do not look beyond, and pause to question. It becomes so much a part of our nature that sometimes we are not even aware of this.

The energy of amassed (or depleted) external power converts easily into the energy of emotional blockages. Morphing very quickly into jealousy, frustration, and anger, we feel it flare when others experience what we want, or as our own desires increase and remain unfulfilled. This keeps the "will-wheel" of agitation and incompleteness forever grinding. Driven by jealousy, vanity, or just plain greed, many people get so passionate about achieving those trappings of external power that they direct all energy and focus to obtain them. We admire and value our physical beauty and may spend hours primping before mirrors or in beauty salons. Having ascended a few rungs on the corporate ladder, we then devise vicious and unethical schemes to quickly climb higher. Our pursuits can be single-minded and obsessive. Driven by insatiable desire for external power, we fly like arrows straight for our self-aggrandizing goals.

Now here is the irony. Most of us undeniably appreciate and value qualities like love, forgiveness, compassion, kindness, and patience—at least in others, if not in ourselves. Movies with themes that evoke these emotions do well at the box office. Books on these universal themes strike a chord inside us. But do we really get the message? These feelings and experiences are so very joyful, even if fleetingly. Yet, how many of us would be willing to invest the same effort that we put in to amassing external power in order to nourish these values in our character, and share them with others?

Since we are clearly aware of these virtues and appreciate them in others, how is it that we do not single-mindedly pursue compassion, empathy, love, and forgiveness in most, if not all, that we do in our lives? What makes us pause, our intentions flagging well before we have reached for and demonstrated our highest level of goodness?

How many people have felt annoyed, or have hurt a family member or a friend while trying to gain external power? How many relationships have been damaged as a result? How many marriages have broken or turned sour due to power games? We often see pursuit of naked power and greed in the workplace. The competitive struggle for products in the marketplace is often replicated inside corporate organizations, as employees compete ruthlessly against each other. We can see this all around us in the steady stream of unethical practices being reported both inside and outside corporations.

As I watch or read the daily news, I can't help but feel that the true beauty of life has gotten lost in the shuffle, as our mad rush to external power steamrollers along. The reason is that this power gives "visible gains" and makes us feel good and powerful at the material level. But doesn't this move us farther away from spirituality in the process?

Healthy competition is good and gives us the energy, the inner drive, and momentum to excel at whatever we do. Yet, we do not see anybody competing for compassion or forgiveness or unconditional love! If human beings are inherently competitive, then why is it that we do not see intense competition to embrace and demonstrate these qualities as well?

These are uncomfortable questions for some.

This is because love, forgiveness, compassion, and gratitude are qualities of the *soul*. This makes them *our* inherent and natural qualities too, that we sadly choose to ignore. The soul does not have a narrow and selfish agenda to pursue. It does not have an ego that can "get hold" of them and claim them as its very own. Whereas ego is a state of mind that generates only negative emotions—fear and anger are its specialties—not qualities of the soul. These emotions serve as thick blinders, preventing us from looking inside ourselves, beyond the physical dimension, and keep us away from true spirituality.

Only when an inner shift from the physical world to the *awareness* of our inner world takes place, can we experience compassion, love, and gratitude in the real sense. These qualities go hand in hand with a spiritually connected person who does not depend upon externals to fashion his identity. Only then do we no longer need to make an effort to instill them or "practice" them. Only then do these qualities become second nature, and change us from within. Only then do we feel complete.

My Reflections

14
Anger and jealousy unplugged

"Holding on to anger is like grasping a hot goal with the intent of throwing it at someone else; you are the one who gets burned."

Buddha

Most of us have experienced anger in one form or another. We're more than a little familiar with the different ways of expressing anger—screaming, thumping the table, hurling insults, and even being physically violent against others or ourselves. We recognize physical and physiological symptoms associated with this strong emotion. We all know that anger affects us physically, and can cause long-term damage to our health and our relationships.

The strange thing is that we usually end up regretting what we've done or said in an angry state! I call it strange because we normally do not like the outcomes of an angry outburst, and yet many of us fall into this trap as a pattern. Extricating ourselves from this habit remains a difficult quest for many of us.

I myself have experienced this strong emotion. Many years back, when my children were growing up, sometimes they would annoy me so much that I would get very angry and yell. My heartbeat would accelerate and I would lose control of myself. In calmer moments I tried telling myself, *kids will be kids*, I must give them space; but that did not help me much.

What did make a difference was a different kind of realization. After I *woke up*, one day my son provoked me on some issue. As usual, I felt the urge to raise my voice. And then a miracle happened! My voice choked and I was not able to speak up. I felt calm deep inside and none of the other symptoms that I would normally have expected emerged. Suddenly, I became aware of a distinct difference in my reactions. In the calm, my voice had softened and I was kinder in context and tone. I had found a different way of dealing with my anger and my children. I realized that I had "moved on."

Most of us realize that anger is bad for us and that we should control it. Yet almost every time we get angry, we blame it on someone else. We might blame it on our colleagues at work or our children, insisting that they are the ones who made us angry and therefore to blame. Have you ever blamed yourself for your own anger?

But if you think about it, anger surfaces in us only because it is already there *within* us. How can I say that somebody else "made me" angry when it existed inside me all along? Someone simply helped me bring it out into the open. Somebody actually just acted as a catalyst to help me become *aware* of my anger.

And what about jealousy? Like anger, jealousy is a blistering emotion that can ruin our life by contaminating our relationships. We could be jealous of someone else's looks, wealth, knowledge, or "success." As in the case of anger, we might be tempted to say that somebody else is making us jealous. But there is a clear difference between anger and jealousy. We can always try to justify our behavior by blaming someone else for making us angry, but how can we blame others for making us jealous? Perhaps they are living the kind of life we'd always dreamed of. They may not even be aware of our distress and "green-eyed" observation. While we are suffering and feeling tormented, they are simply going along their merry way! Many jealous people resort to rationalization, claiming that the more fortunate person is "flaunting it" and showing off, but most are aware of the other's innocence. Does it not feel strange when we look at it this way?

Anger and jealousy are essentially forms of energy. They are vibrations of a lower level that pull us down. They are very strong negative vibrations that can be diverted or replaced but are difficult to contain. When we try to control them, the pent up energy spews out with even greater force. We may not utter a word in our anger, but when it comes out, it feels like a volcanic eruption.

The question then becomes how to unplug this energy. At its inception, ask yourself this: really, what inside me is making me angry? Take your attention away from the external to the internal, for that is where the key remedy lies. Anger can be neutralized with positive vibrations of love and light, of calm and peace. Say, "love and light" to yourself, and keep repeating this the next time you feel angry or jealous. And observe the miracle!

There is a longer-term solution as well. Underlying anger and jealousy is insecurity—insecurity about losing or not getting all those things and attention that basically give us external power. If we change our understanding of that power—that is, if we look for power inside ourselves rather than outside—we regain the internal security that renders the outer frills meaningless. The trick is to be open to revive our internal power. Such internal power comes over time, with a deepening awareness of connection with the Divine Source. Then anger and jealousy do not hold sway. Their roots unnourished, they quietly subside. In this way, some serious emotional blockages will recede.

When we are on a path of spiritual living, we understand that the people who make us aware of our anger or jealousy are actually messengers from the Universe. Invaluable educators, they are meant to make us aware of these emotions so that we can see through and thus heal them. A spiritually connected person is above strong negative emotions. He is a dispassionate observer of the play of emotions.

My Reflections

15

Attachments unplugged

"Whenever the free and unlimited expression of life and love is prohibited or limited by any circumstance or condition, the soul, which is joy itself, is not fully expressed. Joy not fully expressed is the feeling that you call sadness."

Neale Donald Walsch

I remember as a young housewife, while trying to tidy up my closet, I would pull out everything with the intention of donating or disposing of things. But like so many other well-intended housewives, I'd end up putting them back very neatly, in the hope that they would someday be of use. Of course, that day never came, and things just kept accumulating till the drawers were overflowing. Sounds familiar, right? Why do we cling to things like clothes and mementoes for years and years? We may hesitate to call this clutter, but isn't that what it is?

Compare this to some other simple pleasures in life. We go out to a restaurant for a meal, have a good time, and before long have forgotten about the money we spent, as well as the fun we had. We go on holiday, spend into the thousands, come back happy, and almost immediately our memories begin to fade. Then why do we buy an article of clothing and keep it for decades, even when we have outgrown it?

I remember that when my son was very young, he used to collect ticket stubs for every movie he had ever seen. Not only that, but he would not allow me to throw away empty shoeboxes, even after he had discarded the shoes. I could not see any practical use for these, nor understand his attachment. Interestingly, when we had to move houses and I asked him to pack his belongings, he just picked up some personal things and said that the rest was not useful and could be thrown away. This was almost 80% of the stuff in his room. What a surprise!

While joyful memories may fade, we hold on to our belongings; we hoard them. When we hold on to things and do not remove clutter in the house, we block the flow of positive energy. Things lying around unused in the house are like "dead" things that attract and hold negative energy. Only when we throw away the negative energy do we attract the flow of the positive. It is for this reason that some people find it almost therapeutic when they tidy up their storage bins and cupboards.

I remember a friend who would throw one dress away whenever she bought a new one. She just could not tolerate an "overly busy" closet. Her method made her feel comfortable and light. By releasing the negativity from the drawers or cupboards, she was symbolically also releasing stress from her system. I experienced this myself a few years back when I was stressed about something. Although I did not realize it at the time, cleaning up my household clutter was helping me to de-stress! Today, I know a little more about energy levels and understand how and why I used to feel better after tidying up my closets.

It might surprise you to see how this tendency applies at the mental level as well. Normally, our minds are full of thoughts. The "mind work" just doesn't quit. One thought leads to another: sometimes it plays a cassette of past memories, regrets, anticipated power games against others, and fresh new ways to make the next move in the chess game of life. In seemingly lighter moments, for "kicks," there's always plenty of room for judging, criticizing, and cooking up some juicy gossip that puts others down. So much negativity all around! We hold on to all such thoughts like glue. And by not letting go of some of these thoughts, we end up littering our lives with mental clutter. Like physical trash, mental clutter has the same effect of blocking a healthy flow of positive energy inside us.

At the emotional level as well, a lot of us hold on to painful memories, resentments against people, or guilt for things that we should have or should not have done. When we do this, we also hold on to the negative vibrations that these emotions carry. We hold on to so many fears, so many attachments and passions, so much anger that they bind us and stop us from moving forward. This is clutter of the worst kind!

The Holy Geeta puts it nicely: "What have you lost that you are weeping? What have you brought that you have lost? What have you made that has been destroyed? You brought nothing. What you have, you got here. What was given was given here. What you took, you took from this Universe. What you gave, you gave unto this Universe. Your attachment (to these) is the cause of all your sorrow."

To progress at the spiritual level, we need to remove clutter not only from our homes and our wardrobes, but also from our minds. We need to quieten all the monologues and dialogues that are constantly going on in our head. We also must be willing to release the negative emotions and resentments that we carry deep inside. Only then can we make space for the positive thoughts and emotions through which positive energy may flow unobstructed.

Once we have let go of negativities at all levels, and have quieted our minds, we welcome the positive energy of love, compassion, and forgiveness to flow in. This regenerates and reenergizes us. It elevates us to a newer vibration, which is positive and lighter in density. We feel light and can be in joy.

My Reflections

....

....

....

....

....

....

....

....

....

....

....

....

....

....

....

....

....

....

....

16
Attachments unplugged, again

" Anger will never disappear so long as thoughts of resentment are cherished in the mind. Anger will disappear just as soon as thoughts of resentment are forgotten."

Buddha

In discussing attachments, we looked at our inclination to hold on to our belongings, our thoughts, and our emotions, and how that creates energy imbalances within us.

Let us now look at another aspect of attachment that we often experience. We can be especially possessive in relationships—with our family, friends, and Significant Other, in particular. When we see a close friend making new friends, we might feel ignored, insecure, or jealous. That might occasion feelings of anger or unease. In India, we often find mothers getting into relationship problems with daughters-in-law because of their inability to share their son's love and attention with someone else.

The fact is that all of us experience different kinds of relationships with different people. All my friends, for instance, are not the same. I have various kinds of friendship with different kinds of people with a range of personalities and interests. Why would I feel ignored or slighted when someone I care for and am friendly with makes new friendships?

Would this not be the same dynamic of attachment that we discussed earlier?

Love is not a thing. One can divvy up an apple, and share it, but one cannot apportion love. Love is an unlimited flow of positive energy that is, by its very nature, *inclusive* and not exclusive. Once we understand that love is unlimited, and that loving one person does not reduce love for another, we are better able to maintain equilibrium and security in our relationships. A man can love his mother, wife, and child at the same time. Loving one does not reduce or in any way compromise love for another.

Our inclination is to hold on to people. We expect all relationships to be permanent and everlasting, forgetting that people on different sides of a relationship can grow differently. Many years back, we returned to live in Mumbai after living overseas for some years. I looked forward to meeting up with my old friends again, many of whom I had not seen for some years. Strangely, the reunion of friends was not quite as pleasant as I had expected. I remember being very unhappy for quite some time, because many of the old friends with whom I reconnected had changed. They were not relating to me the way they used to. I somehow expected these relationships to be as I had left them years ago. I recall feelings of disappointment and frustration. I just could not understand what had happened—at times, I blamed myself for their behavior and at other times, mentally questioned theirs.

It was only later that I realized it was I myself who had changed. In the years that I was away, my friends had also moved on, made new friends, and were used to a different lifestyle. It required a sensitively attuned rapport to rebuild my friendships with them. It called for a different kind of relationship. Now, I can see that it was my attachment to expectations from earlier friendships that was the cause of my angst.

We need to understand that people grow at every stage of their lives. Depending upon our personalities, experiences, and exposure, we all grow differently. I have seen this in my own life. I am not who I was ten or even five years back. I have changed intellectually, emotionally, and spiritually. I have learnt to relate differently, even to some of my family members who have also grown differently. I don't feel discouraged or bored when I meet friends and family who are discussing things that no longer interest me. I do not judge them, but remain a silent observer. If I cannot relate to their thinking, how can I expect them to relate to mine? We have simply moved in different directions, all perfectly appropriate and deserving of respect. I feel it is reasonable to accept that sooner or later, everyone will move on in life in different directions. I now understand that it is unfair to pass judgment on others who may simply have developed and grown in different ways.

People grow from the inevitable accretions of daily living, but sometimes circumstances force them to change and develop in unexpected or unusual directions. I have myself seen many changes unfold in my life. My husband and I have lived in many countries. Life in an Eastern country is so different from life in a Western country. With each move, we adapted in the usual mundane and mechanical ways, but also in our roles as husband and wife, abandoning older notions and embracing newer ones. Both of us had to evolve. That is how we grew together, and bonded harmoniously.

On the other hand, I know of at least one couple for whom this adaptation did not happen. Moving across culturally different areas of the world, they could not stay in balance, resulting in the breakup of their marriage. One could guess that each adapted differently to the new situations, and in ways that were not congruent with the other's response. Clinging to past experiences and expectations apparently did not translate well in the new milieu. Marital discord was the unfortunate result.

When such divergence takes place in relationships over time, it can often be emotionally challenging. We may either resent these changes or, alternatively, build new relationships that are better aligned with our new ways of thinking. Resentment against those who have grown differently only brings pain and emotional blockages. Once we understand and accept that life is a river that moves steadily on, and that we need to move on too, we will not impede the flow by hanging on to relationships that have lost their meaning for us.

This does not mean that we break ties with those who have grown differently. It just means that we live and let live, always allowing room for others to grow. We rediscover old relationships if we can, but if not, we let go happily, without rancor.

From a spiritual perspective, unplugging attachments to old relationships that are no longer serving our growth will open us up to new experiences that can be uplifting. Keep in mind that each one of us meets only those people who have something to teach us, or to learn from us, at the spiritual level. Once these lessons are wholly learned, our "teachers" fade out of our life and are replaced by new people, who are going to be conducive to further growth. The path of each individual's spiritual evolution is different. Each is precisely where he or she is supposed to be along that path.

This is spiritual growth that, in the truest sense, may also be called evolution.

My Reflections

....
....
....
....
....
....
....
....
....
....
....
....
....
....
....
....
....
....
....
....

17

Resenting our resentments

"Send love in some form to those you believe have wronged you, and notice how much better you feel and how much more peace you have."

Wayne Dyer

We have discussed different kinds of attachments and the impact they have on our life. Sometimes that impact is clearly discernible; at other times it can be subtle. Our inability to detach ourselves leaves a "residue" in the form of emotional blockages that harm us internally. This effect is generally not apparent on the surface.

These blockages can take the form of resentments against people, events, or circumstances. Resentments often arise out of our unfulfilled expectations of others. If you think about it, meeting anybody's expectations on anything can be very tricky, considering that our own expectations of the same people may keep changing over time. Besides, everybody's expectations for the same person can be quite different. Accumulating resentments for unmet expectations can be truly hazardous! Yet how easily we justify our resentments against those who have hurt us physically, emotionally, or mentally! Often we are not even aware that festering resentments have lasting consequences at the spiritual plane.

One can sometimes read resentment and anger in other people from their facial expressions, body language, or eye contact. Even when traveling in a Metro or a lift, I can often identify people who are carrying the weight of resentments in their hearts, just from the look on their faces. An early morning scowl is a dead giveaway!

At times, we experience the urge to distance ourselves from someone we don't know very well, or whom we've met for the very first time. Have you ever noticed how you feel when you are required to communicate or simply be with a person who is holding on to negativity? Do you sense the uncomfortable vibrations? You may suddenly feel drained when such "carriers" of negative energy are around you. It is almost as if our bodies can sense the heavy load of frustration, bitterness, or vengeance against the world that this person is carrying and emitting. We are indeed very sensitive to energy vibrations.

Resentment in one person can be quite infectious; it can seep out as anger and bitterness, affecting anybody and everybody within range. The negative energy of resentment is especially strong. Negative energy transmits quite rapidly, attracting more negative energy of like vibration, and a spiral can develop very soon. These are very dense and tightly packed. They pull us down and also bring down others who interact with us. Related consequences follow close behind, such as poor performance at work or deteriorating health, which in turn lead to more resentment.

Resentments go hand in hand with feelings of insecurity, anger, emotional pain, and lack of trust in others. Looking at it this way, we realize that when we're resentful, it is because we have lost external power. We want to replenish this external power, and for that we resort to emotional manipulation or revenge. The more we play, the more we lose, because others pick up the negative energy we emit. And before we know it, our most valued relationships are injured.

Longstanding resentments may even become cherished parts of our identity. They offer a false sense of specialness that seems to define us. We find safe harbor in them, afraid to let them go for fear of losing our "special" identity as long suffering victims. For this reason, we hold fast to them, which prevents relationships from moving forward—even when the "guilty parties" are ready to change and make amends. We justify our present behavior with our past experience, ignoring the damage we are doing to ourselves and to others.

At the spiritual level, we have to remember that past events cannot be brought forward in any way whatsoever, and should not be lived in the present. Holding on to *anything* from the past releases negative energy. The same principle applies, whether we are holding on to unpleasant experiences, people, emotions, or resentments; all involve the same dynamics of clinging, and the resultant suffering at all levels.

How do we get out of resentments? One effective remedy can be to neutralize them with positive energy. The first step is to become *aware* of and recognize the undercurrent of resentment in our thoughts and feelings. Becoming *aware* means becoming *present to*—abiding in the *Now*. That step in itself will break the power that this energy has over us. Negative emotions lose their grip once we recognize them and name them for what they truly are. Every time a negative thought surfaces, call it by its name, "Ah, this is my resentment." This alone could break the spiral. The trick is to *let go*. Then neutralize it with feelings of love and light. Rise above it and watch it like an observer, and visualize this process. You will notice that it gradually loses its control over you. Deeper negative emotions may need to be fully experienced—not at this "slow-burn" level, but rather at HIGH heat—and then passed through. In other words, they must be fully exposed, experienced, exhausted and overcome.

Resentment against people who have hurt us also loses its hold once we know love and forgiveness in the real sense. I will discuss this in some detail later in the book.

My Reflections

....
....
....
....
....
....
....
....
....
....
....
....
....
....
....
....
....
....
....
....

18
Slavery of habits

"First we make our habits, then our habits make us."

Charles C. Noble

Some of us are in a habit of drinking tea at particular times of day. So when it is teatime for us, the mind calls out loud and clear, "Tea! Tea! Tea!" And we run towards our cuppa! Some people get into the habit of eating dessert after their meals to satisfy their sweet tooth, or smoking after their meals to relax. These may sound like addictions of the body, but they are really habits of mind.

Many adults cannot seem to get their day started unless they have looked at the morning newspaper. This habit may stay with them throughout their lives. My husband has had this habit for many years, quite like his father. He recently felt he needed to support a "green" idea and decided to shift from the daily paper to a digital format. He downloads news onto his mobile device and reads through it on his commute to work. Even this modest change in habit has become an arduous one. He admits that his mind continues to resist this change, hankering for the tactile experiences of paper.

Once developed, habits take charge and eventually control us. Those who have tried to give up any habit know that habits seem to have a mind of their own. Habits are notoriously difficult to break, but actually, once we divert our attention away from them in a different direction, this becomes easier.

My husband was a habitual "light" smoker for many years. About fourteen years back, he suddenly decided to quit smoking. It must have been initially agonizing. He agrees that his change started with the acute awareness of the hold this habit had over him, and of his desire to break free. Once he stopped, every time he felt the urge to smoke, he would force his mind on to something else; he did not feed this habit with any further thought, and was able to break free.

Many teenagers have experienced the effort of getting *into* the habit of drinking alcohol. Peer pressure often starts this, and it's usually quite an effort to "acquire the taste." I know someone who could not tolerate alcohol and would invariably get an upset stomach and start vomiting after a single drink. But he kept giving it the old college try, trained himself, and eventually did get into the habit of drinking. Gradually, his body adapted to this and stopped its reactions! Acquiring this habit was a deliberate and considerable effort.

Acquiring habits often seems to be easier than getting out of them. The point I am making here is that if we can make an effort to get *into* habits, then surely we can make a similar effort to get out of them. What does it take to do this?

Sometimes, as long as things are working for us, we do not want to change. Only when an unforeseen circumstance comes along, and old habits and attitudes do not serve our purpose or harm us in some way, do we actually make the effort to change. That is why very soon after a heart attack, people are able to make drastic lifestyle changes, whereas nothing could have motivated them to do so before the event.

In a similar way, old *thinking* and *emotional* patterns can be diehard habits—they really do die hard! They become mainstays of our identity and our personality. The good news is that they can also be deliberately and consciously changed and replaced by new patterns when they stop working for us and no longer give the desired results. When we think differently, we feel differently. When we feel differently, we do things differently. This understanding can be a powerful tool for breaking the slavery of habits.

How do we apply this idea to relationships? We often find that we respond to situations from our ego's point of view, and get involved in the usual power games in our relationships. This is a habit too—we may do this consciously or unconsciously, and even with people who are dear to us, including our children.

Many times we want to see a change in the behavior of our children. To do so, we relate to them in a particular way, again and again. And as parents usually discover, this just doesn't seem to work! Most of the time, our expert advice bounces off the wall! Sometimes, it's the parents' behavior that needs to change too. The trick then is to break loose from habitual responses, first by becoming aware of the undercurrent of ego that drives them, and then by dealing with situations or relationships in a sympathetic and compassionate way. When we relate to our children differently, with poise and awareness, we get a different response.

A friend of ours, a very devoted mother, was concerned about the welfare of her daughter, who was at a university far from home. My sense was that the relationship between the two was going through a rocky stage. She would dutifully phone her frequently and exercise her motherly concern. I noted that with the best of intentions, by force of habit, she would open the conversation with, "So, what are you doing?" I thought her tone might be somewhat interrogative and intimidating to her daughter, who could well have wondered if she was trying to corner her. If, instead, she were to say, "Hi! Am I disturbing you now? Is it a good time to chat?" and then sustain that openness throughout the conversation, an ego-free relationship could perhaps develop. Small as it may sound, this change would respect the personal space and privacy of the child, giving her a choice as to whether she wants to talk at that time or not, and is non-threatening. This change in the dialogue, in its tone and content, would essentially require a change in Mom's habits. It would require a change in attitude, and, most importantly, awareness.

Similarly, the move towards spiritual living involves changes in habitual modes of dealing with people, events, and situations. To move from a material way of life to a more spiritual way of life, some old habits and assumptions have to die, and new ones take their place. It is a question of making conscious choices and using free will to make the change.

A shift in perspective moves us forward. We could start with an awareness of the play of our ego in all that we do, including the seemingly passive stranglehold of attachments and resentments, and how they are blocking our spiritual growth. We need to break free of these bonds! Instead of looking into the negatives of life, we can train our mind to look into the positive; we can replace complaints with gratitude. Make living in faith your new habit. Make living in gratitude a habit. Make positive thinking a habit too. Once these habits are assimilated, living a spiritual life can itself become a habit.

My Reflections

19
A spiritual fight for freedom

"A mind which is possessive will be possessed. To possess anything is to be possessed by it. The more you possess, the more slavery you create around yourself. The freedom comes when you unlearn possessiveness."

Osho

As individuals, when we hear the word freedom, the first thought that comes to mind is the ability to do whatever we want without anybody's interference. According to my Web dictionary, freedom is "the power or right to act, think, or speak as one wants, without hindrance or restraint." This is in the context of the material or physical world. In this context, our freedom would mean being able to obtain and use the things we need or want in this world, whenever and however we want. Many of us cherish this right. Some often take it for granted. However, at a different level, freedom is a key step to spiritual awakening, even though it may not be immediately apparent.

Do you notice that sometimes we buy things for our comfort but end up being a slave to them? People become obsessed about their homes, cars, and electronic gadgets. They can feel very angry and miserable if their things get damaged or stolen. We not only possess things but also sometimes hoard them, becoming so attached that they literally *own us* instead of *we* owning them. Now that doesn't sound like freedom, does it?

Then there are those who wear their wealth on their sleeve, in a manner of speaking—like a vanity marker plate on a brand new car. They derive most of their joy from admiring acknowledgement of their possessions. In this context, freedom also means not seeking identity, or social and professional status, in owning possessions.

Freedom from attachments of this kind automatically includes freedom from a plethora of negative emotions. Not having the desired material objects, or fretting over their maintenance, often gives rise to anger, jealousy, fear, resentment, guilt, blame, pride, and frustration. Sometimes, one single negative emotion can take charge of our life and seem to rule and control our every act. It affects us as well as others we interact with including our families and those around us. Think about it: if I don't have designer diamond jewelry, a luxury car or a fancy home, and have no particular desire for these either, why would I feel jealous if I see my neighbor owning them? Once I experience this freedom, I would barely notice what others have. Freedom from all such negative emotions is the essence of real freedom.

Things that we identify strongly with give us external power and self-esteem. Lack or deprivation of these sources of external power sometimes leads people to addictions or even crime. Living as an alcoholic, a workaholic, or a shopaholic are some of the more painful and conspicuous ways that addicts seek to fill the power-void. When we are not attached to the physical world, with its frills and laces, or to the world of popular opinion, with its praise and accolades, it follows that we will also not have addictive habits. Freedom from *addictions of all kinds* then is real freedom.

We feel deprived when we desperately want a circumstance or a thing, and don't get it. Usually the feeling of want will impel us to take steps toward feeling complete inside. When the stomach is full, we don't need to eat more. But when we are hungry, the urge to eat is uppermost in our minds; it blanks out other thoughts and concerns. It drives us forward. In corporate America, they have a nice-sounding name for this: incentives.

In the same way, when we are feeling complete because of our connection with the Divine Source, there is no burning desire to possess or own anything in the material world. One does not miss anything, so there is no question of feeling deprived. I don't feel deprived of designer diamond jewelry, or a ritzier car, when I don't even desire them. Freedom from feeling *deprived* in every sense underlies true freedom.

At the spiritual level, freedom has a totally different meaning. Freedom does not mean that we stop enjoying our possessions, or no longer derive satisfaction from performing well in our career, or that our livelihood must suffer. We work for and enjoy what life gives us. Spiritual freedom means that we do whatever we do in an objective and detached way. It means that we do not require externals to give us power, and that regardless of our "net worth" or popularity quotient, we will carry on contentedly with our lives. If we lose some of these things, so be it! Perhaps it was just not meant to be with us. It does not disturb our inner peace.

When we carry on with our life without attachment in this manner, we can achieve what we want in a relaxed way, without any stress. We can perform better in our lives, as whatever we do is with faith and assurance that the Universe is looking after us. We do our best in the situation that we are in, give it our best effort, and then surrender to the will of the Divine with a deep conviction that He will give us what is best for us.

That is *real* freedom!

At the material level, when we pray, much of our petition—after we have prayed for the well being of loved one—is for material gain and pleasant circumstances that would enhance identity and the self-esteem born of external power. If we remain at this level, our shopping list keeps growing in a never-ending spiral. At the spiritual level, we pray will be for freedom from our attachments, our vices, and our delusions. We will pray for freedom from our negative emotions—a very liberating experience in itself.

It can thus be seen that at the physical level we ask for more, and at the spiritual level we ask for less. The physical level binds us to the more; the spiritual level gives us the experienced of total freedom.

My Reflections

....

....

....

....

....

....

....

....

....

....

....

....

....

....

....

....

....

....

....

20
Fear of the unknown

"Love is what we were born with. Fear is what we learned here.
The spiritual journey is the relinquishment —or unlearning—of
fear and the acceptance of love back into our hearts."

Marianne Williamson

The next time you are fearful, ask yourself this question: *Exactly what am I really afraid of?*

Some would have difficulty putting their finger on the answer. Is it fear of losing all that we possess—our possessions, our wealth and properties and our reputation? Is it fear of losing friends and family that we care for?

If you look closely at these questions, you will notice that the answers to all these questions have to do with external power. We live in fear and worry about being deprived of any of these. This is because we identify with them and feel our existence and self-esteem depend on them. They seem to make up what and who we are.

Or is it fear of something we don't even know, the uncertain tomorrow?

I recently asked a friend how things were after her son's recent marriage and she said, "So far, so good." She seemed to have reservations about her happiness, I thought! Now what does that mean? Even when things are going fine and life has given us whatever we need, we hold our joy back because we fear losing it. We don't trust that the Universe will continue to work in our best interests and, at some level, we believe that we must zealously "guard" our happiness and good fortune. This defensive posture, we believe, serves to mute our rejoicing, lest we attract the jealous energy of others. It may also be adopted to evade "Bad Luck," perceived as always lurking in the shadows. The idioms "keeping our fingers crossed" and "knock on wood" speak of this superstitious and untrusting relationship to life.

We need to be mindful of the Law of Attraction that powers our every thought—positive or negative. When we fear something, we attract the same kind of experience that would validate what we are thinking. And then we say, "See? My fearful thoughts were 'right!'" Actually, we were not thinking "right." We simply attracted those feared events!

The philosopher Descartes is best known for his famous dictum, "I think, therefore I am." I understand this to mean that the mind informs us that we exist, and gives us our sense of identity. Let us look at it another way. Our thoughts shape our emotions and physical structures and symptoms as well. Thoughts of fear cause the symptoms we've all come to know, such as knots in the stomach, perspiration, and irritability. On the other hand, thoughts of love and compassion rejuvenate us with calm and peace, and give us a welcoming demeanor.

Fear is the heaviest and the densest of negative vibrations. In fact, all other negative vibrations stem from fear. In other words, the root cause of any negative emotion, such as guilt, jealousy, and anger, is generally fear. Only in our deeper, quieter moments, when we actually remove all the layers of negative emotions, do we realize that the deepest underlying factor is *fear*.

Sometimes my husband wakes up in the middle of the night, worrying about our children who live overseas. He says he fears for their safety and welfare. I have to frequently remind him that mentally sending them love instead of worry and dread will benefit them as well as us. By changing our thoughts from fear to thoughts of love and gratitude, we attract a different experience in our lives. We will be able to feel the difference faster than you can imagine.

We fear losing our life. We fear death because of our fear of the unknown. Some people live in fear their whole life. What a way to live!

Someone I've known for many years has always imagined the worst for himself. He sees a snake where there is a rope, in a manner of speaking. He has planned his entire life and major life decisions around fear. Every move, every measured and unsure step, has been hobbled by this complete lack of trust. To be sure, he has prospered materially, yet his fearfulness continues! This fearfulness has affected not only him but also his entire family. All these years, it has looked and felt as if they were walking on thin ice. I can only wonder how difficult it must have been for the family to live in that fear, year after year.

We do need to tackle or, better yet, to pass through our fears to be able to grow spiritually. The presence of this negative vibration in our beings can be a serious stumbling block to spiritual awareness. Because fear is a negative vibration, it needs negative thoughts to feed on and survive. The moment we neutralize our fears with love, affection, and prayer, its power starts to recede. Reducing fear in this way uncovers the space for joy and compassion to emerge. Only when faith and gratitude flow into our life does fear disappear.

Having said that, I acknowledge that it does take some effort before the demons of fear leave us. This is because even when we pray for peace and calm, we sometimes do so in a way to test our new thought patterns. Will it work? How long will it take? Only when prayers are offered in total faith, not with any expectation, but with firm acceptance of an outcome for the Highest Good, can we see the results. The results should not be expected but accepted as they manifest. We are not the ones to seek or "see" results, as that implies an expectation, an "ownership," a role as a 'doer'. In reality, we are not in control of the results. Results always come on their own, as and when we attract them. It is ours to simply accept them as an offering or a blessing.

Has anyone ever feared losing the love and compassion that lies at their core? We fear the loss of things that we acquire and inherit, but we cannot fear losing qualities of the soul—qualities that we were born with, inherently spiritual and pure. After I "woke up," fear of death and many other internal fears just got "flushed out" of my system. It is indeed a great relief to experience the state of being cleansed, as if some heavy weight has been lifted off, and to live in this joy and freedom.

My Reflections

....

....

....

....

....

....

....

....

....

....

....

....

....

....

....

....

....

....

....

Part Four

BELIEFS

The Baseless Binders

21

Superstitions—as you believe it

"The root of all superstition is that men observe when a thing hits, but not when it misses."

Francis Bacon, Sr.

It has been said that the way to change human behavior is to change the underlying beliefs. Our beliefs—what we believe in individually and collectively—are what control our lives and drive our decisions and actions.

Sometimes very rational people act in a way that seems irrational. However, what may appear irrational to some may in fact not be random or crazy at all, but a very deliberate act inspired by beliefs that we call superstitions. These beliefs, as is true of all beliefs, are of course not based on verifiable fact or actual experience. The difference between superstitions and ordinary beliefs is that superstitions seem to be even further removed from familiar causality. Yet, they give us temporary reassurance in magically addressing our problems. They may give us a sense of confidence about our decisions and choices, or may prevent us from doing certain things out of fear.

Most superstitions have been followed over long periods of time and passed on from one generation to the next, as folklore, hearsay, and cultural takeaways. As a child, I was told not to wash my hair on

Thursdays, as this was considered unlucky for my brothers. It still does not make sense, but I have followed this diligently through the years. I was surprised recently to find out that my adult daughter, who has had a Western education and lives overseas, also defers to this injunction intuitively. This superstitious belief appears to have been passed on to her unknowingly.

In India, we have a lot of do's and don'ts that we derive from omens, and accept as messages from our gods. Over generations, many of these have taken on the power of unwavering beliefs. Political leaders follow them, communities follow them, and individuals swear by them. If superstitions were true and scientifically proven, people would believe in the very same ones in each and every culture. There is of course a strong cultural influence in the genesis of superstitions. Each culture has its own distinct set of them, along with its own reasons for perpetuating them. I am in no position to judge whether any of them are true or not, or whether they should be followed or not. But I understand that it is the *energy of our faith* that drives our beliefs. If we look closely, superstitious beliefs are validated and supported only by our faith in them.

We do not realize that we ourselves actualize those omens by the force of our energy—be it positive or negative. If we truly believe in superstitions, they are likely to prove true for us. By the same token, if we do not energize them with strong enough thoughts, they lose their force and do not become our reality. We therefore have the power within us to prove them right or wrong, and that power lies in our faith and consequently our *thoughts*. The power of thought should not be underestimated. And that is the key to overcome the power of superstitions.

Once while I was on a holiday in India, my driver suddenly stopped the car on the way to the railway station. When I asked him the reason, he said that a black cat had crossed our path which we, as well as others the world over, consider a bad omen. And then, without another word or batting an eyelid, he immediately restarted the car and continued the journey. This was his way of mitigating a bad effect or risk, "cancelling" the omen, thereby evading, in his mind, what he was sure would lead to an unforeseen negative consequence.

Did this really help us to avoid an accident? I don't think we could have avoided one if it had to happen. But by stopping the car, he (and I) changed our thought pattern, perhaps averting a bad experience. Stopping the car symbolically changed our thinking; we put the cat "behind us" in our thoughts and hence too, a bad experience.

Similarly, just before I was planning a long trip to Europe, I read my horoscope. It did forecast some long-distance travel for me, but also indicated sickness during my trip. We all know how difficult it is to control such a thought once it has arisen; it seems to assume a life of its own! Every time I would think of my trip, almost instantly, I also thought of what my horoscope had said. So I decided to neutralize that fear. Whenever the thought of illness popped up, I replaced it with a positive thought. I would say, "Love and light to my fears." As it turned out, I had a very good holiday with no signs of illness. I'm convinced that had I continued to entertain thoughts of sickness, I would have definitely fallen sick, as I would have driven my thought energies in that direction and attracted some kind of physical challenge.

Superstitions hold powerful sway over people who live mainly in the material world and feel distanced from the spiritual world. Seeking support and protection from "outside" forces to give them confidence, they overlook the One Presence and Power that can actually do so. For those who are spiritually inclined, superstitions hold no meaning. Their source of strength comes from the inner world where faith, gratitude and prayers are their lodestars. They get their confirmation and validation from the Divine.

My Reflections

....

....

....

....

....

....

....

....

....

....

....

....

....

....

....

....

....

....

....

22

Ah, if only my luck would have it

"Declare yourself a non-victim of hate, ill-luck, destiny, sorrow, disaster.... Roar the Truth—I am the child of the Lord. He can never deny me!"

Swami Chinmayananda

How many times have we heard people say, "It is not my destiny," or "I'm just not lucky enough"?

People get many things that they aspire to in their lives. Some call it dumb luck, while others see it as their entitlement, since they have put in hard work. When they don't get their way, most people click into the mental blame game: it could be bad luck, somebody else's fault, or that popular standby—"circumstances beyond my control."

It seems that we wobble on a weak foundation of uncertainty and disbelief. We are often uncertain about getting the outcomes that we strive for, and do not believe that things will always work out for us. So when good things happen, we feel really lucky! Conventionally religious people thank "the Man Upstairs" for His preferential treatment, while unbelievers thank Lady Luck.

Think about this difference between living in *uncertainty* and living in *faith*. Faith is the conviction that whatever is happening is happening for the best, even in uncertain or difficult circumstances. It is an internal knowing that the "best" is part of an unimaginably vast jigsaw puzzle, wherein we cannot see all pieces at the time, but know they are continuously finding their rightful places. But if, instead of faith, we have extreme skepticism or disbelief, we will worry about the consequences and live in fear. There is no trust that the Universe will always provide what we need. That is where the concept of luck comes in at the physical level.

On the physical plane, when knowledge, focused action, and clear intention are combined in any endeavor, we get our results. However, sometimes even these factors are not enough. Things may not work out despite our best efforts. When this happens, it is because whatever we are doing and intending is not aligned with our life's larger purpose. It could also be that the time is not opportune for us at the spiritual level. Only when our intentions and our actions synchronize with the Divine plan can we be led to our goal. Some also call this destiny.

When I was at a teacher training college in New Zealand, I was made aware of the different learning styles of students, and different teaching styles of teachers. I internalized a very important concept at that time: when a student is not learning, it often isn't because the teacher cannot teach, but is usually because the teacher's teaching style and the student's learning style do not jibe. Sometimes we teachers had to try out various teaching techniques and styles with different students, to facilitate learning.

At the spiritual level, we can apply the same principle. When we do things that are not in line with our life's purpose, the Universe, as the wisest and kindliest of teachers, keeps trying to alert us by throwing different experiences our way until we learn. At the human level, sometimes these lessons are easy to understand, and sometimes difficult. We need to remind ourselves that everything that happens is designed to nudge us in the direction we are meant to move in spiritually. Finally, when the Universe's teaching style matches our learning style, we grasp the higher lesson, move forward, and evolve to the next spiritual learning.

When I look back at my life in this light, I clearly see the truth in this statement. If you look back at your life too, all of it, with the pleasant and the unpleasant parts, and connect the dots, I believe that you will find it too—the imprint of the Universe as your teacher.

There are no mistakes in the Universe. To me, this is stating the obvious, yet it is such a sublime Truth that we all need to keep reminding ourselves of it. This is the very foundation of spiritual faith. The Universe all around us seems to work according to an exact and elaborate plan. Nature itself, as we can observe it, is a good example of this. The same applies to our lives. Only when we have completed the spiritual lessons at every stage of our life will we move on to the next level of our learning experience. That is the cycle of spiritual evolution that all living beings go through.

On the worldly plane, we seem to have simplified this profound truth: when the Universe's teaching and our learning styles match, we consider ourselves lucky; when they don't, we consider ourselves unlucky. We do not realize that we may be unlucky from the human perspective, but that the experience might be a part of the larger design and be "just what the Universe ordered" for us to grow at the spiritual level.

Many of us thank God when things are going well, but forget to be grateful to the Divine when we have an unpleasant experience. Now that sure demonstrates faith! Some months back, my friend's daughter was heartbroken when her fiancé broke off their engagement. She was understandably very upset and blamed first herself and then her destiny. When her tears had subsided, I told her to thank the Divine Source even for this experience, as surely there would be something better in store for her. Sure enough, within a few months she had found her soul mate and is now happily married. She realizes now that in fact the earlier negative experience was a blessing in disguise.

It requires courage, faith, and wisdom to adopt this approach. The fact is that we overlook a lot of good things when they come to us easily. We take them for granted. We claim them as our right, as if we are entitled to everything that is good for us, and all the time. But then, when the negative hits us, we blame God or consider ourselves unlucky. If we can receive good things with grace, then why can't we accept negative experiences with gratitude? In both cases we need to acknowledge the hand of the Divine! If we receive good things with arrogance, then we will not learn to accept negative experiences with humility.

Let us examine this carefully. Our negative experiences are intended to weaken our ego and bring us into gratitude, humility, and even surrender. This is a key step in our spiritual journey. How many of us actually understand this important truth? A spiritually evolved person will find a blessing in every experience, for at the spiritual level all experiences are only positive. There is nothing negative.

When we say we are not lucky, we are actually showing ingratitude for what we have been blessed with. When we say we are lucky, we attract more reasons to feel blessed, as that is the message and affirmation we are offering to the Universe. To be lucky, we have to *be grateful*; we have to *feel* the abundance.

At the material level, we consider ourselves lucky when we have everything we would like to have, and continue to get. At the spiritual level, it is a blessing and grace to realize the connection and feel the all-presence of Divinity within ourselves and in everybody around us. Being lucky or unlucky loses its meaning at that stage, as we are in joyous surrender to the Divine Source.

My Reflections

23

Idol worship

"The truth is that God lives amongst his people, and is not found in stones."

Sant Kabir

Temples in India have a rich tapestry of idols representing the Hindu pantheon. It is common to see devotees in fervent prayer in front of these idols. They inspire enormous faith and devotion. Worshipping idols seems to be a form of prayer that many of us are comfortable with and that is widely prevalent.

I have often wondered why we pray to idols. What power do stone or metal statues have that we bow our heads in front of them, make offerings of fruit, flowers, and even money, and leave our petitionary wish lists at their handcrafted feet?

In ancient times, people prayed to various physical manifestations of nature—celestial objects like the sun, the moon, and other natural elements. All these objects were perceived to be "super-natural" or basically representing a power higher than us. Later, some civilizations deified these natural elements, which eventually were given more recognizable names and forms that we see today as idols. Clearly, these idols or deities are not physical manifestations of the Divine, but *representations* of what we perceive the Divine to be.

A common thread through the ages has been human faith in the natural universe as the Provider. We look up to the starry heavens when we face difficulties in our daily life. We seek inspiration and solutions from above in matters that are essentially human. Idols are forms meant to symbolize different soul qualities that we as humans can recognize and relate to in our lives. Each physical feature we see in a "graven image" is meant to represent a particular quality we aspire to, or associate with the Divine. The Hindu pantheon, for instance, is rich in such symbolism. This is why people in India have different deities to whom they pray at different times. Faith in their particular deity's potential to grant their specific wishes is intense and unshakeable.

Idols of our chosen god can help us focus and quiet our minds. They help us pause the continuous flow of thoughts in our minds so that we may contemplate something higher than ourselves. Sometimes, before we enter a temple or a church, we are stressed, anxious, or emotionally disturbed. However, the moment we enter the place of worship and stand before an idol, we often experience a particular stillness, a feeling of serenity. I can get this feeling in many such settings: a quiet Hindu temple, a Buddhist *vihara,* as well as a church or cathedral. The idol reminds us of the larger purpose of all Life, and renews our faith in the benign presence that runs our lives. We quiet the mind, removing at least temporarily all the conflicts churning inside. And in that moment, we must remember our connection with the Divine.

It is of course true that some of us, as devotees standing before our decorated idols, do not think beyond what we see in front of us. Even as we pray to them, we remain ignorant of the symbols and attributes they represent. This can be a missed opportunity for deeper spiritual realization.

When we show reverence to a statue, we subconsciously demonstrate faith in what it represents. It is our faith in the Divine that we lavish on the idol. When we pray to idols and surrender to the will of the deity, we in effect, pass on the positive energy of our thoughts and faith to the Universe. I believe that this energy of faith comes back to us as blessings, naturally fulfilling our wishes.

This energy balancing works in another way as well. When people come to a temple, they may either come to thank the Divine for granting their wishes or to ask for something. Those who come to express their gratitude leave their positive energy at the temple. My sense is that other people who may come needing their wishes to be fulfilled then pick up this energy. In this way, all energy finds it equilibrium.

After my awakening, I started praying to a formless Divinity. God-names no longer mattered. I began to feel the presence of the Divine in everything and everyone, with or without idols. That is what attracted me to the word Energy, which I learnt in Reiki to represent the Higher Source of all life. Of course, I could not visualize energy in the way I can visualize idols. I cannot touch or see it. But I can feel it, like the air I breathe. I know it is there; else I would not be alive. I simply experience it to remember the formlessness of the Divine.

My Reflections

....

....

....

....

....

....

....

....

....

....

....

....

....

....

....

....

....

....

....

24
Rituals, customs, and traditions

"They perform all sorts of rituals, but they do not obtain liberation through them. They wander around the countryside, and in love with duality, they are ruined."

From Sri Guru Granth Sahib

I grew up in a religious and ritualistic family. My mother would often take me to temples and faithfully follow religious customs, traditions and rituals. She also has a small prayer room at home, her own little corner with idols of her favorite deities, colorfully decorated, where she prays fervently every day. During my childhood I would often join her—we would prostrate before the idols, light a small oil lamp, and chant mantras. On certain days, we would be fasting. On other days, we would feast before or after the prayer. Before eating ourselves, it was mandatory to "offer" some sweets to the deity. That was a key ritual.

In India, we follow a lot of rituals—all in an effort to please and appease the gods. We believe in them and we think they bring us results. As a child, I did not understand why we followed those rituals but I never questioned them. It's now clear that I accepted them blindly, following instructions that had come down to me through generations.

People diligently observe customs and traditions that may be thousands of years old. Many religions have them as their defining features, which have become part of their cultural identity. As a result, at some point these customs and traditions seem to merge with religious rituals.

The island of Bali in Indonesia, advertised in their tourist literature as the "island of Gods," has some very charming customs. If you drive or walk down busy markets in downtown Denpasar, you will invariably see Balinese ladies, dressed in their traditional dresses, carrying intricately designed and colorful baskets of incense, fruits and flowers into the miniature stone idols placed along the shop entrances, quite oblivious of the traffic whizzing by.

Sometimes, customs and traditions need to be questioned, so that their true intent is understood. When we follow them unquestioningly, or feel bound by them, or when they are performed out of fear, things can take a different turn altogether. That is the time to pause and reflect.

Performing rituals unconsciously, by rote, takes us away from our real spiritual purpose in life. We generally see the practice of rituals as an important part of our culture, but the Universe doesn't operate on the basis of rigid do's and don'ts. It doesn't care if we drop the incense burner or forget our evening devotions. Spiritual practice is more about detaching from worldly matters to turn our attention inward, toward our vast inner selves.

I began to better understand the value of rituals after my spiritual transition. There is no harm in chanting hymns or mantras—they take our mind away from all the monologues and dialogues that are going on inside our heads. Chanting mantras helps control our mind and discourages it from wandering. The mind stays in the present, free of past regrets and future fears. However, chanting a memorized verse is different from chanting with feeling. When people chant with feeling and faith, there is a difference in the vibration, and it touches them from the inside out. There is a feeling of oneness in the immersion that is difficult to describe or rationalize. Some people get tears in their eyes while chanting, almost as if they are in communion. That is the power of devotion, and at that point of Unity, chanting becomes an affirmation of their faith.

Similarly, when we prostrate before the idols, we symbolically surrender our ego. Surrendering the ego leaves behind humility. Humility is the sine qua non for receiving grace from the Divine; it is the foundational state for spiritual growth. We can meditate, we can be in faith, but if we are not humble, we still have numerous lessons to learn for our spiritual growth.

In the same way, there is nothing wrong in occasional fasting—it is said to do our physiology very much good! It teaches us discipline and self-control, giving bodily processes a well-earned holiday. However, sometimes we see people fasting as a religious ritual and at the same time thinking about food and missing their favorite treats. If our thoughts are stuck in food all the time, then we are better off not observing the fast.

There is no harm in offering flowers and fruit to our deities – these can help evoke intense feelings of devotion and surrender in an expression of love for the Divine Source. The key is not to repeat rituals and traditions mechanically, without understanding and without feelings of faith, devotion, and surrender. If done with faith, they can actually be helpful in supporting our spiritual quest. Most important, we should not follow rituals out of fear that if we do not perform them, something will go wrong.

Some people perform rituals regularly and religiously, but they pray with expectations, aquiver with strain and anxiety. However, it is only when prayers are offered with faith that the real channels of communication are open between the devotee and the Divine. When there is fear of any kind, there is little room for spirituality. Where there is love, even rituals or rescuing an ant can bring us closer to the Divine. All roads that are trodden with faith and gratitude lead us to the Divine.

Today, I continue to follow some rituals myself, but with a deep sense of gratitude. I follow them with faith and inner conviction that whatever is happening is happening for a reason. My mind is totally calm, and not skittering around in fear. I am at peace; I am in surrender.

My Reflections

....
....
....
....
....
....
....
....
....
....
....
....
....
....
....
....
....
....
....
....
....

25
Power of attorney over our life

"Eventually we will all understand that all wisdom is within us, and as we remember, practice and access this wisdom, we will become our own best teacher."

Brian Weiss

Whatever our religious persuasion, many of us like to follow a teacher or guru who appears to have some spiritual authority. The teacher could be someone whose knowledge, understanding, or explanation of religious scriptures appeals to us. Individuals who demonstrate "mystic powers" and abilities—mind readers, clairvoyants, and tarot readers—might also captivate us.

It can certainly be helpful to have someone guide us in our spiritual quest. Teachers offer their answers to our spiritual questions, inspire us in our faith, and may point us in the direction of our spiritual awakening. Most of us need someone to elucidate the wisdom in religious scriptures and guide us in our spiritual journey. However, I find that some people tend to lean on their religious leaders for just about *all* the decisions in their lives. It is as if they delegate responsibility for their lives, and those of close family members, to them. No decision, no choice—it could be related to a wedding or a financial investment or something mundane—is made without their blessing.

I do not mean to undervalue the spiritual knowledge or authority of religious teachers. I am referring here to a tendency in some to lead their daily lives completely based on what they are told by their chosen guru. When we hand over the running of our life to someone else in this manner, are we not also giving away the responsibility of our decisions, our choices, and our actions? Remember that we are the ones to bear the consequences of our actions and decisions. Remember too that if we give away our power of choice, we lose the opportunity to learn some lessons through our own experiences. Some of these lessons may in fact be crucial to our inner growth.

When we start leading our life blindly, as directed by our gurus, we may do ourselves spiritual harm. Instead of surrendering our ego to the Divine, which would be the ultimate in spiritual awakening, we are surrendering our free will to our gurus, and letting them take charge of our life and control of our destiny.

This approach can be comfortable for some of us, and does appear to make life smoother. It might even inspire the confidence needed in making the right decisions. But I question again if this allows us to grow spiritually. When someone else occupies the driver's seat, we spend far less time reflecting on the issues and receiving messages or guidance to follow our instincts. We could be ignoring the wisdom that the Universe imparts to us directly.

In that sense, we are all by ourselves in our spiritual journey. Each flower has to bloom on its own; each candle has to be lit individually. Each soul has to find its own path in our spiritual journey.

My Reflections

26

Religion and spirituality—
where do the two meet?

"For me, the different religions are beautiful flowers from the same garden, or they are branches of the same majestic tree. Therefore, they are equally true, though being received and interpreted ...through human instruments equally imperfect."

Mahatma Gandhi

For many people, religion plays an essential role in their spiritual journey. Religious faiths that people follow depend on many factors, such as the country of their birth, their family traditions, and perhaps their culture. Some people make a choice about their religion later in life, not staying with the faith they were born into. They make this choice when they go deeper into themselves and seek a religion that inspires them and answers or satisfactorily addresses their most pressing questions. They may find guidance and solace in reading scriptures, steadfastly following their rituals and rules, or attending ceremonies in a place of worship.

All religions offer a path to the same Divine Source. How then do we reconcile the variations in practices and interpretations found in diverse religions with the singular nature of Divinity?

The principles underlying all religious teachings and Holy Scriptures are, I believe, essentially very noble and point to the same divine direction. The problem comes when people of one religion believe that their religion is superior to another, or that their religion alone can lead its followers to *God*. This belief is sadly responsible for continuous interpersonal conflicts, wars, and crimes throughout history. I don't believe that such conflict is the true intent of any religion, nor can I reconcile these ideas with my understanding of Divinity.

The moment followers of any one religion believe that their religion is the *right* one—the only one—I think they have lost it. The moment a religious leader thinks that his precepts are the best and the only ones, he has lost the larger purpose. Then the ego is raising its head in its glory, misleading the group to believe that their religion is the *chosen* one—the one that offers the only path to spiritual growth. The ego, seeking strength and validation in numbers, then urges them to convert others to join them, sometimes even forcibly. The result is an external power game, which is the complete antithesis of spirituality.

One might also find groups or sects within a religion putting other sects down. Sometimes devotees of a religious group vie with each other, trying to be "better" devotees by racking up more donations, for instance. Giving high amounts does not make one a better devotee, and competing with others definitely defeats the very spirit of spirituality. In spirituality, there is no competition of ego. There is only unconditional and universal love and compassion.

The dynamics of ego are such that it does not give up and leave us easily. We can see it shifting from the material world to a religious world, strange as this may sound! A deeply religious person could be living in complete seclusion or immersed in charity work, singing the glory of the Lord, but if his ego has not at least subsided, then has he really grown spiritually? Some spiritual leaders may believe that they are better and more worthy than others, even within the same faith. I have some difficulty understanding this, for in spiritual matters, how can any person claim to be better than another, whatever the breadth of their knowledge, when the resident Spirit is the same in all beings?

Each one of us follows his own spiritual path. It is a wonderful inner journey to self-awareness. We follow it at our own speed, in our own time. One person could be more evolved in one aspect of spirituality, while another could be more developed in a different aspect. Eventually, all lessons will be learnt by everyone—some will learn sooner, and others later. Different degrees of learning are of course experienced by each soul in each situation before it reaches *home*.

Spiritual knowledge can be conveyed and shared. One can *try* to communicate this awareness to others. But I believe that spirituality has to be experienced individually. The *knowing* that comes with that experience surpasses the knowledge that is gained from books or religious leaders. Words, expressions, and language structures can never adequately express the experience of the unique connection with Divinity. Sometimes I feel that we can study and debate endlessly to understand intellectually and explain the wisdom we understand, but each one has to experience the connection himself; we can at best describe the flower, but each one has to smell the fragrance himself.

It is only through a spiritual experience that we can know how this connection feels, how it changes us from the inside out. That is when the limitations of self-esteem and external power become evident, and we see them as binding constraints; that is when our ego starts to lose its power and humility steps in. That is when we move beyond the intellectual understanding, and embody the purity of the feelings of love and forgiveness; that is when feelings of gratitude and surrender become a way of life and a way of sustaining it. This is my essence of an awakening.

In this journey, can religion and spirituality meet? Yes indeed, religion can help us, support us, and explain spiritual concepts to us. But when we look at religion not as a means toward spirituality but as an end in itself, we lose track of our own purpose. We can stay within our faith and be spiritual. However, it might surprise some to know that this journey may be possible even without support from a religion! In this realization, spirituality is the means as well as the end. Spirituality is an experience of inner growth that changes our perception of everything around us. It touches us at all levels and reaches us through our heart and the mind. There is tremendous power in the faith that comes of that merger with the Divine Source. Some might call this "communion."

My Reflections

27

Knowledge—from science to spirituality

"It would be possible to describe scientifically, but it would make no sense; it would be without meaning, as if you described a Beethoven symphony as a variation of wave pressure."

Albert Einstein

When we speak of knowledge, generally we understand it more in terms of worldly knowledge of that which can be studied, observed, and empirically verified. Human quest for knowledge has indeed resulted in remarkable progress in many fields. We have understood a lot about how our body, our planet, and the billions of distant galaxies work. Scientific progress has come in a torrent of discoveries; opening up frontiers in ways that our ancestors never thought possible. They would have regarded these developments as supernatural! And this process of discovery continues at an exponential pace. It has been said that all that we regard as supernatural today is that which is yet to be discovered and understood.

How does this dovetail within the spiritual context?

Consider this: Thinking is what drives discoveries. There is a *thought* behind every scientific discovery that has ever been, and will be made. Thought is what triggers and sustains our enquiry that in turn leads to inventions. The object of our learning and the thinking behind it are closely related, in a way that is not immediately apparent. Everything is pure energy, and only when the thought catches the vibration of its goal can it be realized and executed. This is what makes discoveries and inventions possible—synchronized vibrations of our thought and the goals it pursues.

To achieve this, we of course must have the technical skills, focus, and commitment to our objective. We need to act consistently, and with perseverance. Most of the inventions in the scientific world were not made in a single bound. They required continuous effort and patience, along with the faith that we could do it and that *it could be done.*

If the potential did not exist, it would not have been possible for humans to send man to the moon. If it were not possible to discover the cure for a disease, say, malaria, we would not have even thought about it; we would not have been able to direct our mind to discover the cure. These achievements were possible by human beings because the *potential* already existed. We just (re) discovered it.

The same principle applies to spiritual knowledge. If it was not possible to connect to the Divine Energy and there was no potential for this at all, nobody would have ever reached that stage. Absent the wisdom of saints and sages who, through their meditations and prayers, received grace from the One Source, the Wisdom of the Ages would have had mainly to do with comfort and survival. The potential existed, and the techniques and inspirations they followed led them forward in their spiritual quest.

Spiritual experience may be described as *synchronized vibrations of our heart and Divine Energy.* Synchronized vibrations are what convert mere potential to observed reality. Everything is energy, vibrating at different levels. It is possible to realize those inner discoveries and experiences that are already potentials within all of us. Spiritual knowing is as much available to us as scientific knowledge. All we have to do is rediscover and reconnect to it. The only difference is that it is knowledge that has to be *felt*, not necessarily reasoned. It is knowledge that comes through our *heart*, together with our intellect. And unlike static concepts that are laid down in books, spiritual knowing is ever flowing and ever growing.

In the immortal words of Swami Chinmayananda, "The path by which you can realize the Truth is not merely dry intellectualism. Your intellectualism must be sweetened with devotion and reverence; your heartfelt emotions must be reinforced with knowledge. The head and the heart must merge together. Contemplation is not an intellectual comprehension or an emotional appreciation. It rests on the two, like the two wings of a bird."

This is our predicament as human beings. Our mind has always been an asset to our progress. At the same time, it is also a serious obstacle to our spiritual awareness and evolution. We are so used to grabbing hold of everything with our mind that we want to understand and possess spiritual knowledge also through our mind. When we cannot "get it" in that manner, we are disinclined to believe in it, as the rational mind needs to see verifiable facts, and empirically observe them at the material level. At the spiritual level, facts are not initially apparent to the naked eye or to the enquiring mind. Yet it would be fair to say that potential for spiritual discoveries similarly exists, waiting to be remembered!

Scientific discoveries generally come after years and years of perseverance and commitment. Our inner journey also needs commitment and persistence, but with the direction turned inward. The Universe inside of us is as vast and spectacular as that which we see outside of us. Only when the mind has been quieted with practice and perseverance do we actually become open to participating in this knowledge, through the heart, through our intuitions and instinctive messages.

Spiritual knowledge has to be felt or experienced, not just thought about. Yet even this element is not "one size fits all." To fully experience spiritual knowledge, each one of us has to determine his own size and contours via his own life, his own intentions and actions, his prayers, his faith, and his own feeling of gratitude to the Divine Source. The menu of options is wide open!

Knowledge at the worldly level makes one very intelligent and yes, knowledgeable—it does indeed have a useful purpose. But if it remains unchecked, it can only boost our self-esteem and ego. On the other hand, combining great knowledge with conscious living can play a remarkable balancing role and can make one humble. It can have a grounding effect and change the person, from within. It leads us to the authentic experience of spiritual knowledge.

Spiritual knowledge is not something that is separate from us. It is not something we "work on" or "aspire to" for an hour a day. It cannot and should not be divorced from all the worldly roles we play in our day-to-day life. It can, rather, become the foundation of our being, of our sight and of our breath. Absorbed by every cell of the body, it cleanses us and changes the way we live. The hallmark of spirituality is that it is lived, not performed as one of the routine and required activities in life. Only then does a person experience real joy.

My Reflections

....

....

....

....

....

....

....

....

....

....

....

....

....

....

....

....

....

....

....

....

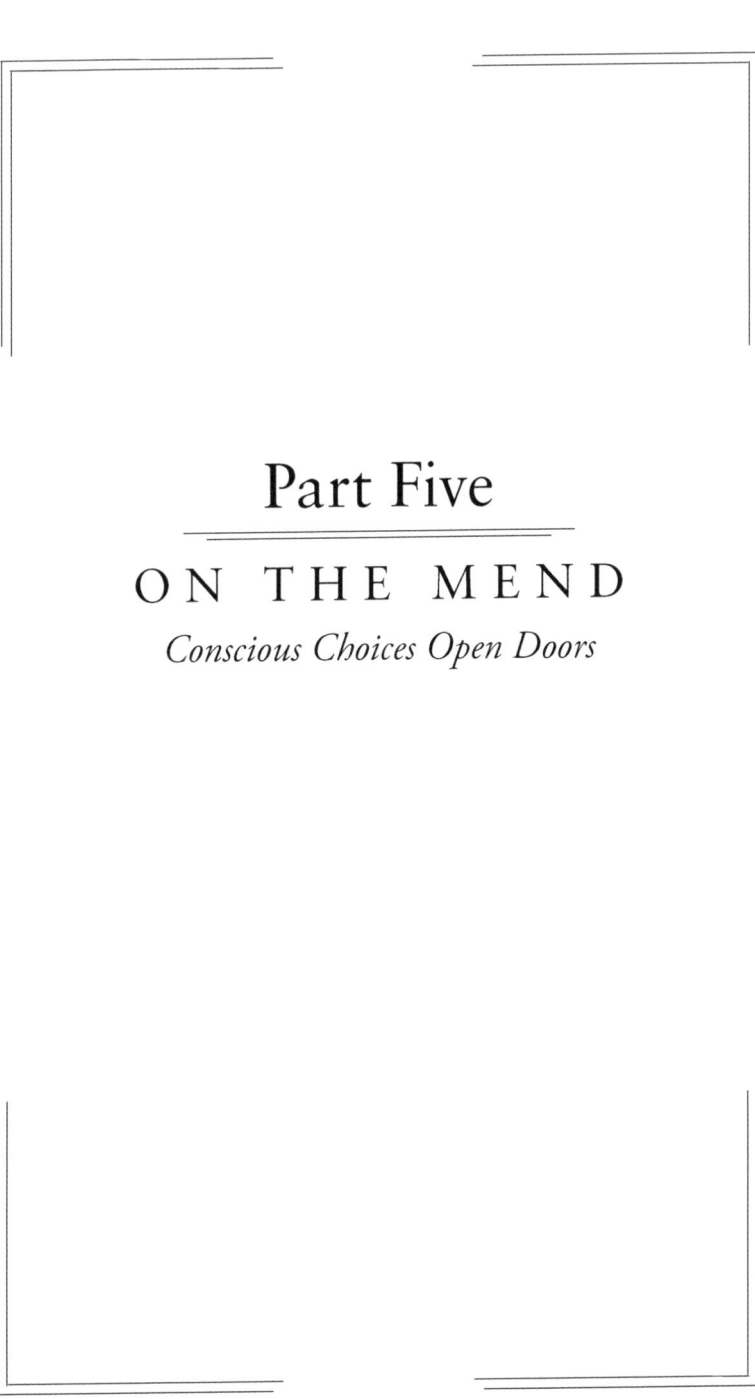

Part Five

ON THE MEND

Conscious Choices Open Doors

28
Going with the flow

"If you say you will not move into sadness, that you want only happiness, then you cannot flow. Flow is only possible if you accept everything as it is, unconditionally."

Osho

My husband tells me that today I am very different from the person he married many years ago. I tell him the same about himself! This is probably true of most of us, whether we are aware of it or not. Even when we know that change is inevitable, many of us have trouble accepting all the changes that come into our lives. And this affects our growth, in particular at the spiritual level.

Change is a law of nature. Sometimes we see it clearly around us—seasonal changes in the color of leaves, for instance—and sometimes we don't, as when changes take place inside our body. When we grow in years, we also grow physically, mentally, and emotionally. Change occurs at a hormonal level as well as at a cellular level. These changes incline us to behave and react differently in different situations, as well as in similar situations at different times, depending upon our mental, physical, and emotional stage of "the game."

How we respond to changes at all these levels *is the essence of* our spiritual journey and evolution. In every situation, we need to reflect, asking ourselves if our response is mainly to satisfy our ego, or whether another response might be possible. For instance, could our response be arising out of compassion? An honest determination would indicate if we are taking the opportunity to grow spiritually—or not.

We can adjust to change in either of two ways: by accepting it or resenting it. When we accept change without fear and with open arms, the process becomes easier. As we adapt to change, as we go with the flow of the change, our own energy vibrations become less dense; we become lighter, and make the change a positive learning experience. The Universe supports us in a way that makes transitions easier. Ways just open up for us, and we can feel the strong supportive hand of the Universe at our back.

I remember a time when a friend of ours lost his job some years back. He was in a foreign land, with a wife and children to support. Concerns about livelihood, bills, and supporting his family were surely uppermost in his mind at that time and possibly a source of mental stress. Yet, we were amazed at how stoically he faced the situation, not letting it get him down. Instead of fretting, cursing his luck, and complaining about life or the future, even as he continued his search for another job he could be often found at his favorite golf course. Calm and composed as always, he would joke that he would never get so much free time once he got a job, and wanted to make the most of it!

I found his positive frame of mind truly remarkable. And sure enough, within a reasonable amount of time he got a job and was back to his hectic work routine. I thought this was an outstanding demonstration of going with the flow of what the Universe offers us. This kind of harmonious attitude is what molds the support that one can receive from the Universe.

Living in connection with your inner world gives a particular kind of strength. I have experienced this directly, following a serious deterioration in my health in recent years. Exhaustion is the first thing I feel when I wake up in the morning and this continues through most of the day. I am at a point where I am more or less homebound, as I have no energy to work or socialize. My husband and I have adapted our lives around this condition, as I just cannot cope up with more fatigue than what I am used to. Medical professionals have advised me that there is no treatment for the chronic fatigue condition that I experience, only management. Yet they prescribed anti-depressants to help me cope. I laughed when I was prescribed these. How could these pills substitute for my prayers that I constantly live in? Emotionally I am as balanced and stable as ever. I do attribute this to my continuous connection with the Divine. I am so happy that I learnt about my condition only after my awakening, as probably I wouldn't have been able to take it as well earlier, and might have resented my condition!

Resenting a change—be it loss of a job, move to a new city/country, or any other unwanted situation—gives us a totally different experience. Rejecting or recoiling from unforeseen changes that come into our life affects us at all levels—physical, emotional, mental, and spiritual. Our own body and physiology become stagnant and heavy; our thoughts disturbed and distorted by many troubling questions, all of which exacerbate our fears and insecurities. Emotional reactions quickly follow—anger, sadness, depression, and even guilt—and take control of us. These then have a cyclical effect on body and mind. When there is a non-acceptance of change—which is to say, of the *present moment*—we make the process very difficult for ourselves as well as everyone around us.

No stage or situation in life can ever be permanent. Some people fall into a depression as they age. They miss the fun of their childhood or vigor and excitement of lost youth, forgetting that every stage in life is not only transient, but also full of potential. With age, some of us will develop sickness, disease, or some kind of physical limitation while others may just "drop the body" when its usefulness is over. These are inevitable in our physical transition, and we cannot really control these events.

But the most important element is one we *can* control—how we *react* to the new conditions. These reactions bear not only on our outcomes at the material level, but also on our spiritual growth and journey. If we resent our sickness or our slowness, we will reinforce it, and find it even more difficult to cure. Our own immune system, all riled up with inflammatory anger and frustration, will not be supportive of any treatment. Until we *accept* the treatment deep inside mentally and emotionally, we will not *receive* it physically.

It is a commonly accepted fact that our non-acceptance of and resistance to change is what converts our pain into suffering. It follows that if we accept an illness, then it will not translate as suffering. We will go with the flow and get the support of the Universe in our healing. We will attract the right kind of doctors and treatments, and move on with our life.

Most of us find it difficult to cope when an illness attacks us and we must live with some limitations as a result. People who resent their illness are likely to suffer more. On the other hand, those who meet it with acceptance find new ways to deal with it, and find joy in it. I know someone who started making stuffed toys when she was bedridden. She excelled in making them and reached a point where she could sell them. She had found her peace in this. Some people take their illness as an opportunity to enlighten their spirit, going deeply into meditation and rediscovering the Divine. These are the ones who find their condition to be the proverbial blessing in disguise. Simply accepting the consequences of certain physical limitations, which may be due to an illness or any other circumstances, can create peace within.

The first step in this direction is to accept the change and the *present moment*. Not forcing our way when things are not supportive is a means to spiritual growth. Going with the flow of change, and neither resisting, nor resenting it, makes life a truly rewarding experience.

My Reflections

....
....
....
....
....
....
....
....
....
....
....
....
....
....
....
....
....
....
....
....

29
Being true to ourselves

" One of the truest tests of integrity is its blunt refusal to be compromised."

Chinua Achebe

A key factor in spirituality is integrity. This is not just about being honest—honesty is usually viewed as being directed towards others—but about integrity in our own life, toward ourselves. It is about being true to ourselves.

Some of us lead two lives, one before the public eye and one that is private. Our public life is what we project to the world, with a kind of mask, where makeup is not just on the face but also in our language, in our behavior, and in our attitude. Our private life is the one that is full of our fears, our desires, our self-esteem issues, and our deeper feelings.

We usually like to project a public persona that would seemingly make us more likable, more lovable, and more acceptable to others. But do we always say what we really mean? Do we say what we really think and feel? Do we abide by the principles that we believe in? If not, then we are leading a "double" life.

With a double life comes double trouble—in the form of emotional baggage. People who lead this kind of life build up stresses and anxieties at the sub-conscious level. When they say and do things that are not congruent with who they really are, they carve a distance between themselves and their conscience, leaving something like a vacuum bubble inside. As this bubble grows in size, they need outside support to feel complete. They may feel like fish out of water, as their self-esteem depends entirely upon what others think and say about them. At every step, they measure their identity according to how others are regarding them. Hence, their increasing need to project what they are not as they continue to suffocate behind the mask.

The interesting thing about this phenomenon is that most of us *know* what we are deep inside, even if we do not reflect on it or articulate it. When we meet people "mask to mask," we measure and judge the outer projection of the other person against our inner self, which is our real self. This increases the gap between what we *really* are and what the other person's mask reveals. The greater the gap, the more painful our inner feelings will be. More effort is then required to fashion a better mask for ourselves. And the more the effort, the larger the bubble becomes, and the cycle continues.

It can indeed be very painful and disconcerting for people when they choose to live a double life. We can hide our true self from others, but how can we hide it from ourselves? The more people hide their true self from themselves, the more it haunts them, clamoring for expression.

Sometimes a whole life may thus be spent behind a mask. The more they're untrue to themselves, the further do they drift away from spirituality. This creates a disconnect, a filter, between their true self and the way they experience the external world as well. And that has profound implications for their spiritual journey. Only when their inner and outer worlds reconcile and synchronize can they reduce the heavy burden of guilt and fear that they are carrying. Only when the masks are dropped and there is no difference between their personal and public life can they open themselves up to spiritual wisdom and inspirations.

How do we to recognize this gap in ourselves?

An undesirable experience could one day come along, making us aware of the double life. When that happens, some people simply collapse under the weight of the stresses that they have put on themselves. Some people learn the lesson when a painful relationship cracks this gap wide open, and all outer layers tear and fall apart. They then learn, in the hardest of ways, to be much truer to themselves. A less painful way may be through reflection and introspection that brings this gap into awareness. Once we recognize this gap, we can regenerate. Then we could turn over a new leaf, projecting to the world our *real* self. We could then feel our spiritual light within us.

All masks begin to fall away once we start living at a higher vibration and feel the Divine connection. We then accept ourselves, as we are, grateful for what we are and what the Universe has blessed us with. We are grateful for life itself! We are *in joy*.

My Reflections

....
....
....
....
....
....
....
....
....
....
....
....
....
....
....
....
....
....
....

30

All you need is love

"To truly love people I have learned that I need to let them be, and to love and accept and appreciate them as they are (free of my projections and illusions) and not as how I would like them to be. This is equally true for loving and accepting oneself."

Buddha

The Beatles were on to something when they sang the song with this title. In a spiritual sense too, love is *all there is*. Love not just for others, but first and foremost love for ourselves.

How many of us actually look in the mirror every morning and say to ourselves, "I love you!"? Instead, most of us are on the lookout for some minor flaw or defect of face or form, the wrinkles or the hair, ever disapproving of ourselves. Not loving ourselves distances us from the True Source and results in low self-esteem. This leads us to use external power in our dealings with others as a way to feel complete inside.

People associate love with different feelings—infatuation, intrigue, passion, sex, gratitude for parents, warmth for siblings, attachment to our children, cooperation between husband and wife. Spiritual love is another dimension. It changes the way we look at the world and ourselves. It makes us love and accept ourselves the way we are. This is the love that one feels after experiencing a strong connection with the Divine, even if it is just a fleeting glimpse. It is love that flows very naturally in us for everyone and anyone, a love that knows no boundaries. It is love that comes from inside our heart and is totally selfless. Such love makes us feel wholly complete from within.

I have always loved flowers and admired their beauty, their colors, and their aesthetic effect in the garden and in the wild. Yet, it is only after my move toward spirituality that I have actually *felt* the life within them. I have started touching them in a way I had never touched them before. I have started feeling the communion of love in my touching them, and their touching me, that I had never experienced before. I now feel a deeper connection as I caress them with both hands and heart.

It is a similar kind of love that people often feel for animals; it is the same kind of love that one feels while holding a baby in one's arms. It is unconditional and caring, and even if only for a split second it is free of all expectation. After all, what "concrete" benefits can we expect to get in return from a flower, a pet, or a baby?

Somehow, we do not seem to apply the same principle in regard to our fellow human beings. Recent history is replete with eruptions of hatred and war. This situation would change dramatically if we were willing and able to give unconditional love to our fellow humans. What an unimaginably lovely world it would be if we could see and feel that kind of love in everyone, including those who have caused us harm, who have hurt us, humiliated us, and made us feel small. When we see in others the same life force that flows in us, animosities end and forgiveness falls on all like a gentle rain. It is then that we will feel—and *be*—Divine love.

Considering the way people fight and play ego games with one another, forgiveness seems to be the exception rather than the rule. It is perhaps the most difficult virtue to practice, for in the immortal words of Alexander Pope, "To err is human, to forgive divine." And while most individuals give it lip service, the majority simply cannot bring themselves to lose themselves in the simple act of forgiveness. This is said to be because of the hurt and underlying painful emotions. Agreed! Yet, more often than not, it's because our ego is involved. The issue here is not about forgiving others because they deserve to be forgiven.

The real issue is about ourselves, about *our* need to be released from all the resentment that we are carrying. It is important to realize that forgiveness is the most liberating of all spiritual experiences and a true expression of love. We owe it to ourselves to feel this liberation, and the attendant elevation in spiritual awareness.

A simple technique that I use can have a magical effect. Whenever I have a negative thought about a person who has hurt me, I neutralize it with a positive thought and a feeling of love. This seems more difficult than it really is! I find that over time, my positive vibrations toward that person becomes stronger, and the impact of the negativity decreases and finally loses its hold.

When you apply this technique, not only will you be liberated, but you will have a positive effect on the other person as well. Because we are all bodies of energy and all connected with one another, our vibrations are shared. Loving vibrations of a forgiver are easily picked up, inspiring change in the behavior of the newly blessed one. The relationship then improves or harmoniously dissolves. Forgiveness releases us from all negative feelings that we were holding against people, and has a remarkably cleansing effect on us. Resentment and anger, previously too heavy to unload, simply vanish, and we are free.

Forgiving others is often easier than forgiving ourselves when we have hurt someone, or done something without being true to ourselves. We may have known that what we were doing was wrong, but continued doing it for temporary relief and faux gain of external power. Once we realize that we have made a mistake, the pain can be intense and enduring. Prayers to the Divine, in the spirit of ego surrender, can help release us from this burden of guilt and repentance.

When we are on a spiritual path, love just streams out of us and through us. Love for ourselves brings a lot of inner joy. Then, nothing else is important. We befriend and even love the pimples and the wrinkles on our face; the streaks of grey hair lose their importance. We love ourselves the way we are. We also love all life around us with all of its experiences; we feel complete and blessed to be graced. We feel at one with the Divine!

My Reflections

....
....
....
....
....
....
....
....
....
....
....
....
....
....
....
....
....
....
....
....

31
Do we really need all the answers?

"The whole message is to get beyond the mind and then everything is crystal clear. Then you don't ask any questions. You simply act out of your clarity, out of your transparent vision. And each of your acts has a beauty—tremendous beauty of its own. It has a grace. And it has a power of blessings to shower over the whole world."

Osho

The other day I heard a very nice comment, "When you are aware of being spiritually connected to the Divine Source, you don't have any more questions; you only have answers."

That is exactly how I felt after I "woke up." Come to think of it, however, just why do we need to answer spiritual questions at the physical level? Do we really need answers to rationalize or justify our faith with our mind? Do we need answers to give ourselves external power, so that we can control what others and we do at the human level? How will answers affect our *present* experience?

When we live in this world, we have a natural curiosity to find *all* the answers—about this life, the afterlife, and even our past lives. We want to interpret our dreams and understand omens. We want answers to everything that our limited human mind can imagine.

In our daily lives, we often live on edge, not knowing whether what we are doing is right or wrong and fearing the consequences. Wrong choices may create feelings of insecurity about the future, and uncertainty as to the results of our actions. They may spark emotional or ethical conflicts within us.

In reality, before we make any choices, we generally already know instinctively whether what we are doing is "right" or "wrong." We know it in our bones. Yet sometimes there is an inner clash, a clash between the Divine and the so-called devil in us, between our head and our heart. To our peril, we end up ignoring that instinct, that "small still voice within."

When we do not have faith in our conduct, and make decisions that are not in accord with our personal integrity, we end up with a nagging unease that is sometimes hard to explain. We may then run to astrologers and fortunetellers to predict our future, and to assure us that our choices were right. We may listen to the fortuneteller and relax in temporary respite—until we get to the next choice, and the next.

Astrology and numerology are considered sciences today. I am told that a good astrologer can look at the position of the heavenly bodies at the date and time of birth and predict key events in our life. For many people, this provides some of the answers they need in life. I think that what we do with that information is much more interesting than the predictions themselves, and that brings us back to the issue of choice. Let's say an astrologer predicts that a couple is destined to have three children, yet they decide not to have a third child. Does that change what the astrologer predicted? Was the astrologer wrong? Or does it simply mean that we do have some control over our choices, and thus our destiny?

And if we do control our destiny in this manner, then why do we need these prognostications in the first place? How good is that information for us?

One thing we have to remember is that the Universe is going to show us the right path in one way or another. Decisions to satisfy our ego and to build our identity using external power are not going to lead us "home." We will encounter one experience after another—some easy, some difficult—until we learn the lessons that we need to learn for our spiritual growth. That is the process we all have to go through for our spiritual journey, whether we are aware of it or not.

The spiritual journey can be made difficult or easy, depending upon the choices that we make, using our own free will, every instant. We have to bear the consequences, whether positive or negative, of all our thoughts and intentions, our words, and our deeds. Some refer to this process as the Law of Karma.

When we begin to *wake up and live consciously,* we do not need answers as we go along with the flow of life. Whether things are happening the way we would have liked at the worldly level or not, we have faith that the Universe is looking after us, and that eventually all life experiences will move us toward our spiritual goal. Life brings ups and downs for everyone. Problems at the human level are in fact just spiritual learning experiences and, for the spiritually inclined, they are golden opportunities for ego-surrender. We no longer have questions. We do not *need* any answers and we know that we will be guided to the right path. We become like a river that flows easily around obstacles.

We ask questions and want answers that seem intellectually correct and satisfying. We use our brains to understand and "grasp" everything, forgetting that if we want answers from the Universe, we need to shut off our mind; the mind has to be quiet and clear of any past filters and thought patterns, otherwise the mind can become a serious obstacle to our spiritual growth! Ironically, we try to understand the *Truth* using only that. Real answers come from our heart, not our head. Answers are apparent when the mind has lost its identity, when the heart and the mind have synchronized and merged. That is when the flower of the Divine Truth unfolds within us and life is seen to have new meaning.

My Reflections

32
Dealing with duality

"A peaceful life does not mean a life free of toil and suffering, rather it means living without being swayed no matter what happens. This is a state of true peace and happiness."

Daisaku Ikeda

Duality is necessary to life in this dimension. Where there is happiness, there is also sadness; where there is love, there is also indifference; where there is light, there is also darkness. These are the contrasting "opposite" sides of our dualistic life. Throughout our years, we find ourselves moving from one side to the other in wild pendulum swings, for reasons that we cannot usually understand. As if on a seesaw, sometimes we're up, "on the top of the world," and other times we're down, down deep "in the dumps."

As human beings it is normal for us to relish our pleasant experiences and appreciate what we like. But problems set in when we get attached to anything at the level of ego. When we like something, we like it so much that we want more and more of it—we are uneasy and angry till we get more. And when we dislike something or somebody, we dislike it to the core—total rejection, total non-acceptance, as if the very presence—or even the very thought—of someone is painful. Our heartbeat may even increase at the mention of the offender's name. Our vibrations and language "rise to the occasion" to express these negative emotions.

It's only natural that we get attached to our happy emotions. We do not generally realize this, but it is this attachment and identification with the "high points" that eventually causes pain when the seesaw suddenly plummets to the "low points," or even "hits bottom." You would have noticed, that the higher the upswing of exhilaration, the more painful the downswing of negative emotions when things go crashing down.

A spiritual person can see right through the dualities of life. He becomes a dispassionate observer of a *play* that is taking place between those dualities—the strong feelings of love and hatred, absolute likes and dislikes, joys and sorrows. He is not exhilarated when things go in his favor at the material level, nor is he dejected when life takes a difficult turn. He keeps his ego detached from the events, and is able to maintain calm even through turbulence. He has arrived at equanimity, an emotional balance so profound that mood swings just vanish. A spiritually evolved person walks a middle path, needing nothing so strongly that he would lose balance if he did not get it. Nor is he so attached to anything that its loss would be unacceptable to him. He understands that everything has to pass and that nothing can be experienced before its time or against the plan of the Universe. For this reason, strong judgments and passionate opinions simply do not occur to him, and are no longer meaningful to him in others.

His emotions flow smoothly like a river, not like ocean waves at the mercy of the weather—ripples under calm conditions and destructive giants in stormy weather. Compare this to a person swaying in the currents of life; from anger and jealousy at one time to the temporary calm he feels when desires are met. Isn't this person at the mercy of outer conditions, just like the turbulence of the waves?

It is all right to enjoy worldly pleasures, as long as we do not get attached to them. Regardless of the successes we achieve in life, we must not get arrogant about them, but receive them as grace from the Divine. We should thank the Divine Source for His blessings instead of giving credit to ego when blessings come our way. Hence, whenever we get what we want, it should be received as a reminder to be with the

Divine One, and thank Him. Such gratitude can be truly humbling and can ground us. Similarly, when misfortunes come our way, we should bow our heads and look thankfully for the learning there. That requires courage and faith. And that is spiritual wisdom.

A major change came in my life after I began to *live consciously*. It is not that I have stopped living in the material word. Things are there to enjoy. I enjoy everything that the Divine Source has blessed me with, but in a detached way. The desire to accumulate for the sake of accumulating, for the sake of ego satisfaction, for the sake of vanity and "what others think" is completely gone. I buy things when I need them and do not get disturbed if I do not get them. I no longer yearn to be seen in a favorable light—as an especially intelligent or wise or good person. I simply am. Anyone can start this process, through a life of what I like to call *minimization*. Do not need or aspire to have more. Just give up greed. Remember that frustration and feelings of deprivation come only when you *feel* deprived of certain objects and situations that you aspire to. When you feel *complete*, the feeling of "not enough" is not there, as you don't desire anything. And the dualities of like and dislike and want and don't want begin to disappear. You then feel whole.

My Reflections

....

....

....

....

....

....

....

....

....

....

....

....

....

....

....

....

....

....

....

Part Six

SPIRITUAL TECHNIQUES

Lighting the Lamp Within

33
Fake it till you make it

"Close your eyes and visualize having what you already want—and the feeling of having it already."

Rhonda Byrne

Soon after my awakening, I realized the potential power of affirmations as a spiritual technique. Affirmations showed me a way to talk to the Universe directly to seek help, comfort, and support. And I was amazed that at some key points in my life the Universe responded in a sympathetic way to my affirmations, often with tangible results. These personal experiences have nourished my faith in this form of communication.

The first time I started using this technique was when my husband was looking for a career change. At that point in our life, he was facing critical challenges in his career and had to make some far-reaching choices. I was performing affirmations 24/7. The change came in a very unpredictable and synchronistic manner. Looking back, I am convinced that this was surely the result of these affirmations.

When affirmations don't deliver results in the manner and with the timeline we expect, often doubts arise in the mind, on whether it is really working. I remember the case of a young colleague in Jakarta who was seriously in search of a marriage partner and sought my advice. I recommended to her the use of affirmations to help her. After several months of trying it, she called me once to ask if she was making any mistakes in her affirmations, as she had not progressed and was getting anxious. I told her that there were no mistakes in affirmations as a technique. What was important is how she was affirming, and the degree of her faith. She eventually found her soul mate and has happily settled down.

The question she raised is however an interesting one. Should we make affirmations with expectations, indicate specific timelines in these and wait anxiously for them to show results, or should we do them with faith? When we make affirmations, we are in prayer, and the Universe listens and responds to us in its own way. The Universe has its own sense of timing, and sometimes the response may come in a shape or form that we may not recognize or expect. It is very important therefore to keep a very *open* stance in receiving guidance from the Universe. We have to keep ourselves open to all manner of possibilities that could accommodate our wish. When we remove mental blocks that we often carry unconsciously, we also remove potential obstacles in our communication with the Universe. Our faith in the technique and acceptance of whatever outcomes we get give us a clear and unobstructed connection with the Universe. Only in such surrender can we speak to—and be heard by—the Universe.

Affirmations are energy waves that flow out in a direct call to the Universe. The call is not clear when there are disturbances issuing from the mind—a chain of conflicting thoughts, fears, and expectations. Once we start to affirm, we need to surrender completely to the will of the Divine Source. We need to have faith that whatever is happening is happening for the best, though what that "best" is, may become clearer to us only later in life, and might come in a different form than what we thought! The clearer and purer the affirmation, the faster is the result.

Affirmations need not be said aloud, and can be repeated at the subconscious level. You need not be in meditation to make your affirmations, though that would be a good way to do it. With practice, you will remember to make affirmations while doing any of the monotonous chores that seem to fill up our lives.

The language structure of how you express affirmations is important. They should not be expressed as negatives. If you are looking for work, affirm, "I now have work that is professionally and materially satisfying to me." Do *not* affirm, "I need to find a job in the field of..." *Needs* and *wants* remain as unsatisfied desires—things wanted and needed but not experienced. The Universe does not operate by changing that which you say is NOT into that which IS! If you tell the Universe that something is NOT, then the Universe agrees with you! "Nobody interesting ever asks me for a date!" So be it—nobody does! Therefore, it is imperative that you word your affirmations as if you *already have* what you are affirming, not what you want or need. That is why present tense verbs and the word *now* are very important. "I am now enjoying the job of my dreams." This way, you focus on the present and not on the future which, being future, remains in the affirmation's future—never now. The Universe responds only to and as the present, and not to regrets of the past or fears of the future. Do you see the difference? *Fake it till you make it*, and do it with faith—that is the key. But you're not really "faking it." The desired outcome is indeed present right now – you just haven't seen it yet!

I often use creative visualization to accompany my affirmations. In this technique, I visualize what I want in a very clear and lucid way, again and again. For instance, in our family, my husband and I have seen desired behavioral changes brought about in our children in this way. Instead of allowing our thoughts to go toward the negative side, fueling our fears and complaints, we were able to channel them in a positive direction by affirmations and creative visualizations. Rather than spending our energy criticizing their behavior, we relied on creative visualizations and affirmations to seek help and support from the Universe. Results have been miraculous.

How do we explain this? In simple terms, I see both affirmations and visualizations as ways of transmitting our thoughts as energy into the Universe. I see the Universe as nothing but energy, vibrating in all manner of frequencies. Our finely tuned thoughts therefore have a good chance of resonating well with the Universe, yielding the results that the Universe, in its infinite wisdom, considers best for us, at the spiritually appropriate time. How does the Universe respond to us? Sometimes it sends messages through what we call our sixth sense, and sometimes as inspirations to do things we need to do to realize our affirmations. At other times, the Universe may involve us in unforeseen encounters with people or in coincidences that do not appear logical. The menu of options is quite extensive! Either way, it is the Universe guiding us.

Affirmations have become so much a part of me that even in the middle of the night when I wake up, my mind automatically goes toward affirmations, with every breath. For instance, to stay calm and not let my emotions take charge of me in a stressful situation, I affirm, "I am calm, and I am at peace." This helps me stay in that state, does not lead to any stress, and keeps my mind focused on the task at hand. I can feel the gentle support and comfort of the Universe at all times. I feel like a fetus in my mother's womb—completely secure and protected.

My Reflections

....

....

....

....

....

....

....

....

....

....

....

....

....

....

....

....

....

....

....

....

....

....

34
Meditation – doing it or living it

"The Lord sends you disturbance so that you can discriminate consciousness from thoughts, even in that experience of disturbance. With every disturbance the Lord is sending you a reason for meditation."

Swami Chinmayananda

Most of us are familiar with the term *meditation*. It is universally recognized as a tool to relieve stress and to relax. In some faiths and traditions, meditation is also recognized as a spiritual practice meant to serve a deeper purpose—to facilitate spiritual growth.

There are a number of techniques that are commonly used in the practice of meditation. One such method is to sit quietly for up to, say, twenty minutes, and imagine a soothing light or a flower or a natural landscape, focusing exclusive attention on it. You could also focus instead on a single mantra. I have read about various other techniques, one of which involves meditation while quietly reciting a prayer. Some meditators strive to control the mind and not let any thoughts flow. Others take a more relaxed approach, visualizing a vast dome of sky, with thoughts being regarded as no more significant than passing clouds.

When I was first introduced to meditation in a group class, I remember trying very hard to control my mind, opening one eye from time to time to see what others were doing, wondering if they were able to achieve the state that I was expected to reach, and anxiously calculating how many minutes had already passed and how long I would be required to go through this punishment of maintaining my uncomfortable position! As you can see, I had a lot on my mind! My period of meditation seemed unending and pointless.

Today, although I better understand the concept of meditation and what it is meant to achieve, I apply a different technique of meditation that works very well for me. Meditation is essentially a way to control the flow and churning of thoughts, the dialogues and the monologues that occupy our mind at all times. The key word here is *control.* Controlling these thoughts sometimes teases and entices them to come back again and again, getting stronger each time. It is very natural that, according to the old adage, "What we resist, persists!" That is exactly what was happening to me during my meditation classes.

In my experience, redirecting—or rather replacing—random thoughts with prayers and positive affirmations is meditation as well. We can be in prayer at the subconscious level all the time, even while performing our regular duties in the workplace or at home. We will then be in a meditative mode as well. The mind does not wander hither and yon, nor resurrect old grudges, regrets, or resentments. It is not inclined to dwell on fears of the future. In this state, which is the state of the present, the mind is in a meditative mode all the time.

The basic idea of meditation is to stop or tone down mental chatter and be in a state of silent awareness wherein, absent the usual thoughts, one feels the inner world. All this can be realized when we are in meditation, not just for ten to thirty minutes of the day on a meditation cushion, but at *all* times of the day and night. When we are immersed in a feeling of faith and gratitude, we are in clearer connection with the Divine. The mind is relaxed and at peace. That is meditation too!

Here is a simple technique to quiet the mind in short spurts and thus prepare it for meditation at more expansive levels. I have found that focusing on my breath and repeating the words "I am calm" helps put me in a meditative mode. I do this while waiting at the bus stop, a traffic light, or even when a window is opening on my computer screen. This technique serves as a reminder to me whenever I sense my thoughts getting scattered. It helps me to come back to myself and get grounded.

The other day, I told my son before he was going for an academic exam that if at any time he felt he was getting distracted, he should just close his eyes for a second and say to himself, "I am calm." That simple step would eliminate distraction and bring back his focus. On the other hand, if he tried to struggle against the distraction and force himself to get back to the exam paper, he would waste more time and energy. He found this technique very useful.

At any point of the day, when we switch off from the outside world to be with ourselves, we are in meditation. Rather than being an isolated activity that has to be incorporated into our busy daily routine, meditation can become an essential part of our life. Instead of "doing it," we can easily be "living it." When we are in gratitude at all times, and when we are in prayer and affirmations, we are living in meditation and we are in more conscious connection with the Universe. In fact, we are then living "spiritually."

My Reflections

....

....

....

....

....

....

....

....

....

....

....

....

....

....

....

....

....

....

....

....

35

An attitude of gratitude

*"Focus on being grateful for what you have already.. enjoy it!!
Then release it into the universe. The universe will manifest it."*

Rhonda Byrne

Sometimes people who have everything working right for themselves—good jobs, good careers for their children, money and beauty, tend to grumble even about small things. I meet parents who grumble about their children not doing things *their* way; children like to whine about their parents nagging them about their homework; colleagues may carp about demanding bosses. It seems we are not able to handle anything that is not in complete accord with our expectations. Any drift from familiar, desired ground makes us grumble. When there is even a slight change in our circumstances, we grumble, for we do not accept the situation. This also means that we do not accept the *present* situation. We want to live in the past because we value our past, and/or are familiar with it. We want things to be the way we have experienced them earlier.

We resist change because it threatens to hurt our ego, which is, of course, "set in its ways"—ways that define it, and that it is convinced are the only right ways! Indeed, ego insistently informs us that *its ways are right, and all others, wrong.* For this reason, we do not want to change, but expect others to change. That appears easier, and much more reasonable!

When one is on a genuine spiritual path, all complaints stop and gratitude steps in. In my life I have seen amazing changes. For many years, I lived an expatriate life, with servants at my beck and call, a full-time job, and a hectic social life. It was a thoroughly enjoyable period then. Today, I live in a Western country and have none of those. I chose not to pursue a career and take joy in housework. Somehow, this major change in my life did not excite any complaints (otherwise, my husband's life would have been miserable) as I accepted the present with all that it offered. I love the present as it "presents" today! Things that I valued in the past no longer hold meaning for me. I have found happiness in myself. I feel so grateful to the Divine that I feel no resentment of my present situation. This gives me the internal strength and calm and peace, with no grumbling.

Sometimes we grumble because we feel sorry for ourselves, and we want to get sympathy from others. We forget that the only real help and support comes from within, from our acceptance of the present situation and not from outside. We can feel sorry for ourselves and get sympathy from others, but contentment and joy come only with faith and gratitude toward the True Source. Our grumbling takes our attention away from this realization. If we are unhappy about something, our attitude reflects lack of gratitude.

When we get into the mode of gratitude, our grumbling automatically stops. We accept life as it comes and look at past as past without regrets or complaints. We then do not resist our present experience. Complaining and gratitude cannot coexist. It has to be one or the other

If someone were to ask me today what the first step toward spirituality should be, my answer would be to start thanking the Divine Source every moment of his or her life. That is the simplest and the easiest way to start knowing " connection."

Gratitude should be expressed with full devotion. The flow of energy from gratitude is from the heart directly to the True Source. Gratitude changed my life completely after I "opened up." A major change is the deep *feeling* of gratitude to the Divine Source that is behind every breath. Opportunities that I would earlier have accepted as my entitlement I now know as reasons for me to connect to the Divine Source and thank Him. Dissatisfaction and complaints are distant memories. I have never before felt so complete.

People of some religions like to offer a short prayer of thanksgiving before starting a meal. I quite like this practice, adopting it very naturally almost instinctively when my heart opened. When I think about all the people who often go hungry—at least 850 million worldwide, I hear—I eagerly embrace my daily opportunity to "say grace." And there are other very good reasons for gratitude. When we sit down to the simplest of meals, we know there have been many people behind the scenes, who worked to provide us with that meal. And what about our bountiful Mother Nature, who provides us the food we eat? Everything, everything we eat, comes to us as a result of natural processes somewhere else on our planet—processes that are superbly managed by nature, often despite our interventions!

Reasons for mealtime gratitude do not end here. They grow stronger when we think about what happens after we have eaten the food. We may not like to apply our imaginations to this, unless we fall sick, but the processes of digestion, assimilation, and elimination are also miracles of the Divine Source, and just as amazing. A well functioning digestive system, that extracts the nutrients from our food and converts them to the energy we use and the waste we dispose of, is nothing short of miraculous. We have figured out much about how this system works, but that is no reason not to thank the One who designed it!

I have learnt to be grateful for so many other things that I used to take for granted! I have started thanking the Divine for all the love that I feel and receive from my family and friends. I express gratitude for many regular activities that I now see as small mercies: waking up in the morning after a sound sleep on a comfortable bed; reaching home safely without getting caught in traffic. In short, I feel the connection with the Divine Source all the time, and gratitude has become the theme song of my life. Even if I happen to wake up in the middle of the night, I feel His sweet company, and express gratitude for whatever I am blessed with.

When we feel gratitude deep inside, it carries with it a certain peace and calm. This is because when we express our deeply felt gratitude, any complaints or negative feelings we might have at the moment are simply neutralized, and vanish from our system. The way is then clear to a higher vibration, and we attract positive vibrations. The Law of Attraction works like this: when we sincerely thank the Divine Source for what we have, we attract more reasons to be grateful, and the blessings multiply manifold.

When we do not live in gratitude and do not see the hand of the Divine in our life, we end up angry, and bitterly blaming the Divine for things that we consider wrong. We might say, "I prayed and prayed, and what did I get in return?" Note the clear expectation in this. Or we might say, "What did I do to deserve this?"—a "victim mentality" at its bleating best!

I have found that gratitude strengthens faith that whatever happens, happens for a reason, and that the reason is always in our best interest. We have faith that even when things are not the way we want them to be, there is a silver lining that is not immediately apparent but will show itself later. At some point in our life we all encounter experiences that we definitely do not want. When we have faith and gratitude, we accept these experiences as appropriate for our spiritual growth. We go with the flow and do not blame the Divine Source, or "randomness," or other people, for our situations and circumstances. We do not bore, annoy, or drain others with our grievances. We go through our ordeals as learning experiences, and with full attention, and then move on.

Yes, I understand that this view can be difficult to bring into our awareness, especially when we are in the midst of a crisis. Many people like to thank the Divine when life is running along nicely. It takes deeper faith and courage to thank the Divine when bad things happen to us. And that is surely the time to see the Divine hand in every event of our life. With a deep sense of gratitude, we can then feel sheltered and protected. Therein lies the power of gratitude!

My Reflections

....

....

....

....

....

....

....

....

....

....

....

....

....

....

....

....

....

....

36

The power of prayer

"Prayer may not change things for you, but it for sure changes you for things."

Samuel M. Shoemaker

Regular prayer is a norm in most religious faiths. When people pray, they either pray to thank the Divine Source or to pray for more, with a wish list in their mind.

What is important is the feeling and intention behind the prayer. In India, I've seen people showing anger and using harsh language toward a loved one on the side, even as they are praying. They are praying mechanically and repeating the mantras but are not in devotion. I do not understand the point of such prayer. Where is the mind at that time? Where are the thoughts? And what are they praying for?

There's a vast chasm between conditional praying and praying with devotion. When we pray with expectations, ticking off items on a shopping list, we're praying conditionally—"If I get what I want, it means that God listens to me, favors me, and answers my prayers. But if I don't get what I want, it means that God is dead, God never existed in the first place, or that God is being righteously nasty, and is at fault!"

These kinds of "prayers"—not so much supplications as they are demands—do not really show faith in the Universe, but simply test the capabilities of the Divine, the way one would do with colleagues, relatives, and friends. This is the ultimate in conditional "love"—he cares for me and gives me gifts—therefore, I love him. We see God as a temperamental and manipulable person, *after our own image*, thus bringing Him to a human level. The beauty of the Divine is that even these prayers do not get ignored!

Prayers put us at a higher vibration, and when we do something single mindedly, with faith and devotion, the Universe conspires to realize what we are praying for. When we pray, we should pray with gratitude and faith that whatever is required for us to grow spiritually will be provided, in one way or another. The Universe knows what we need, and we will get it. We need to be open to receive grace. We simply need to surrender.

In my case, along with intense and unshakeable faith in the Divine, my prayers now consist mainly of gratitude and positive affirmations. Sometimes the two merge. So when I want or wish for something, say, a job for my daughter, I do not say, "God, please get my daughter a job!" or "Please help her to find a job!" or "My daughter really wants to be offered this particular job...It would make her so happy!" My prayers are not expressed as petitions, but as affirmations: "My daughter now has a job that is professionally and materially satisfying." Or with gratitude, I might say: "Thank you, Divine Source, for getting her a job that is materially and professionally best for her." I never wait to see whether the affirmations are working or not. I never question them, or peer around corners to see if they are on their way. Rather, I keep going till my prayers are answered. I pray to the Universe as if I have already got what I want. They are spoken with faith that the best will manifest in due course at the opportune time—time not at the human level, as we understand it, but the best time decided by the Universe. That is my faith.

In my younger days I used to pray only when I went to a temple. Now, prayer anywhere and everywhere has become my way of life. I feel the connection with the Divine through my prayers. In my spiritual journey, I have resorted to prayers for guidance, strength, and support several times. I remember a time when a family member had some serious health issues. At one point we had lost hope that she would recover. With the Divine Source's blessings, she did recover, miraculously. I believe that the group prayers that I organized facilitated her recovery.

Group prayer can be an effective technique. It is more potent than one-person prayer because of the magnitude of the higher vibrations generated by more people, who are working collectively. Secondly, it helps the person in need by giving him the confidence of others' support, and his attitude becomes more positive. Since unknown people are praying for him, he also starts praying for himself, and that raises the vibrations that he himself is working at.

Prayers offered with faith in the Divine Source help us survive trying times and give us the strength to carry on and recover. We've all read real life stories of how prayers have helped people to realize miraculous results: desperately sick people who have recovered from serious illnesses, patients whose damaged limbs returned to a normal condition, visually challenged people whose eyesight was restored, and just about any healing situation one can imagine.

Yet, we tend to have a very earthly view of our prayers. When some prayers do not get answered, people may wonder if there is a defect in their prayers. Is God angry with me? Am I being punished for something? Believing that God is unmoved by their prayers, they may lose faith or stop praying for some time. In fact, it is not that the Divine did not listen, or found their prayers deficient in some way. It could be that their mind was full of fears and doubts and expectations that obstructed the flow of pure energy. Perhaps they did not pray with complete faith and in surrender.

Sometimes, people who pray conditionally, i.e., with expectations, stop praying when some negative experience hits them, as they start losing faith in the benevolence of the Universe. By doing this they block out the very source that would help them recover. Are they not losing faith exactly at the time when they need to do just the opposite—have faith and surrender to the will of the Divine?

Prayers have subtle powers. They can guide us along the right path in very discrete ways and give us the support that we need, particularly when we are going through an unpleasant experience. By living in gratitude for all of our blessings, and by being in prayer, open to Divine guidance and making affirmations along with creative visualizations, we can slowly rediscover the positive in our life and in the lives of those around us.

My Reflections

....
....
....
....
....
....
....
....
....
....
....
....
....
....
....
....
....
....
....

Part Seven

SPIRITUAL INSIGHTS
Getting to the "Aha" Moment

37

Letting go of past demons

"Nothing ever happened in the past that can prevent you from being present now; and if the past cannot prevent you from being present now, what power does it have?"

Eckhart Tolle

We often hear people say, "Life isn't easy," or "Life isn't meant to be easy. Don't expect it to be a bowl of cherries, either!" Such people see life as being difficult because they truly believe and feel that to be so. There are others who say that life is good, because that is what they think and believe—despite the occasional practical and emotional challenges all of us face in life. Life surely has serious challenges for many, if not most people. The former are those who are overwhelmed by even the smallest problem, and the latter are the ones who refreshingly keep up their cheer, despite difficulties. What should we make of this difference?

In a sense, we *are* what we believe in, and what we think. In more ways than we can imagine, our thoughts actually do control what we experience and how we feel. If our thoughts remain rooted in the past and in regrets, then our present will also be lived in regrets. And this perpetuation of the past becomes our future experience, an experience of regrets and other negative emotions. In that sense, we *continue* to remain in the past.

When we resent our present, *the now,* we infuse a lot of heavy and dense negative energy into ourselves. Our body becomes very dull and gloomy, affecting our everyday life. This shuts out fresh and more pleasant thoughts and experiences. But in any moment, the option of letting go of our past memories, of opening the doors and windows to a fresh flow of energy, is ever present. A new boost to move forward in a new direction is but a thought away.

Memories of our past can be either good or bad. If they are good, they might inspire and energize us. We remember them fondly and also want to hold on to them. We also want to repeat the same experiences as they are familiar and we feel safe and gratified in them. But this is not realistic, right? Besides, is there growth in reliving the same experiences—intellectual, emotional, and spiritual? Clearly, there isn't.

I know many mature people who take justifiable pride in their past career successes and professional experience. Many base their claim to wisdom on these successes and their age. To their way of thinking, this justifies a repetition of many of their past behavior patterns—these have worked so far, so they must be right. But to my mind, all experiences gained and career successes achieved, without any incremental spiritual awareness, do not qualify as "growth." For instance, if their experiences have included power games in personal relationships, if they were arrogant or have made ethical compromises, then yes, they have the experience. But it goes almost without saying that this experience, even if tagged by the world as "success," does not demonstrate wisdom or spiritual growth.

Unconscious retro living does not allow us to shift in perspective or to develop and refine qualities of the soul. Being "stuck in the past" means exactly that—there can be little or no spiritual progress. Understanding and responding to new situations in the same old way only "digs us in deeper." It is, almost literally, entrenchment! Only when we become aware of a larger purpose in our life, and realize that past experiences repeated without awareness are really not conducive to spiritual growth, do we gain true wisdom. We can develop this awareness ourselves by our own reflections; life's "accidents" also force us in this direction.

When memories are traumatic, as in post-traumatic stress disorder, that is, of course, another story. Horrific memories can haunt and psychologically paralyze us. We may keep replaying the tapes of our past shocks and sorrows so loudly that they overrun the present experience. Some people allow one nasty experience to control the rest of their days, limiting not only their own life, but also their relationships with others.

I remember reading about a seven-year-old girl who had to babysit her two-year-old brother at home. Under her watch, the little boy died in a freak accident. This person, now a middle-aged woman, lives in guilt and remorse to this day. Her tragic misfortune has poisoned her whole life.

In such situations, we need a complete change in perspective to help release demons from our past. We need to develop an awareness of the larger picture of our life and, above all, forgive others and ourselves. The tragedy in this case is that the middle-aged lady has continued to blame herself for mistakes she may have innocently made as a seven-year-old. She has not realized that there is an enormous difference between the knowledge and wisdom of a seven-year-old (in the past) and that of a middle-aged person (present). Looking back as an adult, she does not forgive her mistake as a child.

All of us make decisions based on whatever knowledge we have at a given time. As an adult, we obviously have more knowledge, awareness, and ability than a seven-year-old. We all make mistakes while growing up. But it does not seem reasonable to blame ourselves as an adult for mistakes we made as a child, teenager, or young adult! Once we understand this, we can forgive ourselves and easily dispatch the many demons of our past that may haunt us today. Then we can move on unburdened, inspired by the true spiritual learning that is embedded in the experiences at every stage of life.

We need to remember that the past is truly "dead and gone," and remains only in our thoughts. It is active only when we feed it with our thoughts, again and again. Spiritually, it is of paramount importance to *let go* the past. Try to stop feeding a nagging memory, and you will see how quickly it will stop disturbing you. All we have is *today,* or rather, *now.* What we think now, at present, is shaping our experience of tomorrow. It is ushering in the changes we need in ourselves to grow.

My Reflections

....

....

....

....

....

....

....

....

....

....

....

....

....

....

....

....

....

....

38

Living the future in the present tense

"More important than what is behind you and what is ahead of you is what is IN you."

Swami Chinmayananda.

In the previous section, we discussed the effects that demons of the past have on our present experience, and ways in which we can banish such demons. To fully experience the present, we also need to think about another set of demons—those lurking in our minds about the future.

Many of us like to plan our lives in advance. That seems normal! As teenagers we plan our careers; as adults we plan for our families and try to ensure a good financial situation; and as older adults we think about retirement. We all dream of where we want to be in the future. And we make decisions in the present that may take us to those dreams, based on what we *think* might be required in the future.

Say I have to make an important business presentation in the office to my senior bosses. One approach would be to put all my energy into preparing the presentation—single-minded focus and effort, with faith that I'll be able to give my best, and then not think about the outcome. I could also put in the required work, but with very little faith, and very much fear of the consequences. What *if* it doesn't turn out well? What *if* my bosses do not approve of this idea? What *if* they demote me or deny me my bonus, or, in an extreme case, throw me out of the job? And *if* they throw me out, how will I feed my family? What happens *if* there's a power outage during the presentation? What *if...*? You know what I mean! Before I knew what had hit me, the 'if's' themselves would concatenate into a never-ending chain of Anything Can Happen! The former approach is living in the present; the latter is living in fear of the future, and not enjoying the present.

We cannot live in these "*ifs*!" The "*ifs*" exist only in our imagination; it is only in the mind that we can imagine the unpredictable, and even the impossible. And then we build our lives skittering around those imagined "ifs" and "buts!"

I have often wondered: is it smart to allow the fantasized future to dictate the present experience to such a degree? The future is unpredictable. How can we control that? Many people try to envision as many possible outcomes as they can, along with "battle plans" for confronting, controlling, and maximizing these scenarios to their advantage. But how can we make decisions predicated on hypothetical situations and the unknown? The future is in our thoughts, not yet realized and quite uncertain at best. The present is what we definitely have in our hands. It is at *this* time that we have all the information needed to chart our course. And *now* is the time to choose our thoughts to make those decisions.

In any small activity there are so many factors that could affect its outcome. Imagine that you have to go to the airport to catch a flight. You leave home well in advance, but hundreds of things could make you miss your flight. A normal one-hour drive could take much longer—the car's brakes could fail (because the service last week was done by a novice who was poorly trained); the traffic signals could be out of order, because of a power outage, causing a traffic backup of several hours; uprooted trees may be blocking the way; your driver might suddenly feel too sick to drive, and there may be no taxis available at that hour. Hundreds of contingencies could make your plan go awry and force you to change course.

All of these factors themselves are, of course, dependent upon myriad other chain reactions that could force you to accommodate. The novice car mechanic was a last-minute replacement for a more experienced worker who called in sick; a faulty spare part at the substation caused the power outage, and so on.

Given that the future depends on so many complex and unpredictable factors, mostly unknown to us, how can we plan ahead on the basis of information that is only in our thoughts; when these themselves are inherently limited? How can we expect all of our plans to be fully realized? It would therefore serve us better to fully embrace the *now*, as we make decisions about our future.

We are not in the habit of living in the present. So we try to make all our decisions based on an imagined future, as that is what gives us a false sense of *control*. We spend less time working and living in the present, aware of the information that we do have, and more time imagining and fearing future problems. We generally do not care to wait until we have sufficient information, or the compelling intuition, to make our decisions. Fearing the bugaboo of indecision—said to be *bad*!—we make wrong decisions, not informed decisions. It is these decisions we sometimes regret later, as they were made when we acted out of fear or when the time was not opportune.

We worry about things that will probably not happen, and live in fear that they might. To paraphrase William Shakespeare, "A coward dies a thousand deaths; a brave man dies but once." We then create a series of situations in which we must protect ourselves from those demons that we have created in our heads. Our own creations become our masters! All of our dealings and our relationships in the *present* are then infected with these patterns of fear. We get caught in our own web, just like the helpless spider.

In this way, we create demons of the future, not unlike the demons of the past that we discussed earlier. We might have our plans, but someone else is truly in command. Everything happens at the discretion of the Universe, and nothing moves forward before the *right* time. The Universe already knows the "right" (harmonious and appropriate) time for each spider. When our plans do not match those of the Universe, rest assured that the Universe would, in the best way, nudge us in the direction meant for us.

But don't stop practical planning. Just do it in faith and without fear. As we start living in faith, the influence of these demons starts to wane, and our body feels lighter and less dense. We feel *alive*! Our demons finally disappear when we feel at one with the Divine, when we can feel His presence and blessings in everything.

It is a truly joyful feeling to know, in every moment, that there is a benign hand guiding us, with only our best interest at heart.

My Reflections

....
....
....
....
....
....
....
....
....
....
....
....
....
....
....
....
....
....
....

39
Thinking, living, and being positive

"Watch your thoughts; they become words. Watch your words; they become actions. Watch your actions; they become habits. Watch your habits; they become character. Watch your character; it becomes your destiny."

Frank Outlaw

Facing challenges in life is a given. A child may struggle with her workload of homework. A mother may face daunting challenges to get her child to focus on schoolwork and grades. Sudden illnesses that strike a family member may throw a person into despair and off balance.

You can imagine many such situations and other challenges in daily life, when the mind's reaction is a negative one such as despair, fear, and melancholy. Sometimes a blame game starts, and people resort to blaming themselves or others for their situation.

In such situations, people often advise, "Think positive!" What do people mean by this? Does it mean that when we think positively our problems will go away or get resolved? Yes, that is true in a way, and to some extent! However, thinking positively in a particular situation is just not enough. This can and must become a *lifestyle change* for us to see the magic, the power, of positive thinking.

Any time we have a negative thought, we attract negative energy into our lives. Negative thoughts always lead to negative emotions, which lower our energy levels (you can feel the drop in energy in the body as well!) and put us in a lower vibration.

Energy works in the same way when we channel it into a positive direction. It is by way of our own thinking that we attract the positive and the negative into our life. Thoughts of love and compassion are especially effective in putting us at a higher vibration and protecting us from negative experiences.

There are some simple ways to change the mindset to think more positively. After I started living with awareness, I stopped using the word *if* in my conversations when I wanted to express a possible outcome that I hoped for. In fact, I encourage all my family members not to use *if*, because it implies a lack of faith in the Universe to deliver the best outcome. So when I say, "If I get the job…," I do not demonstrate faith in the wisdom of the Universe that I will get the job that is best for me. The word to use, and to really mean, is *when*. To say, "When I get the job…" means that I *will* get a job, at a time and place that is best for me. I have to wait for that time, with faith, not doubting that I will actually get the job. It is this faith that helps generate positive thinking, and this positive thinking that, in turn, generates faith.

These small changes in our mental makeup take up residence in our psyche, and have long-term consequences for us. For when we show faith, the whole Universe conspires to lead us in the direction that is right for us, for the manifestation of the highest good. The manifestation of outcomes will surely become apparent at the opportune time. It will then be up to us to recognize them.

Positive thought is not enough. We also have to *feel* the faith. And to *feel* positive about life, one has to feel the presence of the Divine in everything. One has to have faith in prayer, and more importantly, one has to live in gratitude. By being positive and behaving positively, we can attract positive energy into our lives.

A positive lifestyle will be meaningful if it is adopted holistically. I could be manipulating people around me, using unfair or unethical means to make money, and then also be "thinking positive" in the context of other life situations. My negative activities will put me in a lower vibration and will not protect me from the negative consequences of my actions. When I am manipulating, where are my thoughts? And when I am playing power games, where are my thoughts? My negative thoughts remain in my mental atmosphere, and I will have to go through the consequences of such thoughts and actions as well.

Thinking positively does not mean that no action is required, or that just by thinking positively and with creative visualizations we can enjoy the outcomes we want in life. Absent a begging bowl, we simply cannot earn our bread by sitting and just thinking sunny thoughts. We do need to act, but with a little change in attitude—with total focus and gratitude, along with the faith that whatever outcome we get will be the best for our spiritual growth. Thinking positively cannot have any effect without the appropriate action on our part. It means that we fully accept whatever result we get with gratitude, as a blessing from the Divine.

Consider the person who lacks self-confidence. That is the underlying characteristic of his personality. He could continue living as the "poor me" and blame his destiny or his introverted genes. Alternatively, he could strive to change himself. That is where being truly positive and the use of creative visualization and affirmation techniques could help create the desired outcome. All these techniques will help to boost his efforts and eventually his confidence. When we think positively and feel positive, the Universe supports us in the positive direction. Thinking negatively and blaming our fate on other people and/or on circumstances weakens us and obscures the ever-present support of the Universe. Unaware of the positive all around us, we remain attuned to the negative.

Being positive means being grateful to the Divine, counting your blessings at all times, and seeing His hand in all experiences, whether good or bad. Being positive means keeping faith in the wisdom and expression of the Universe. Being positive means to live in the *present,* as only when we live in the present can we be positive. We cannot be positive if we are rooted in the past or in the future.

My Reflections

....
....
....
....
....
....
....
....
....
....
....
....
....
....
....
....
....
....
....
....

40

Fine – tuning ourselves

"Use whatever excuse you can to vibrate in harmony with those things you've been saying you want. And when you do, those things that are a vibrational equivalent flow into your experience in abundance. Not because you deserve it, not because you've earned it, but because it's the natural consequence of the Law of Attraction. That which is like unto itself is drawn."

Abraham Hicks

I remember a small and interesting thing from my childhood. We lived in a small town in Northern India. My grandmother lived in another town some 20 miles away. On many occasions, when my mother was sick, my grandmother would show up at our house unexpectedly, asking about her health. She would say that her instincts often told her when something was wrong. As a child I often wondered what this communication was all about. This mystery stayed with me for many years. What or who were these instincts, and just how could they know?

More recently I have read somewhere that animals communicate amongst themselves, with nature and with us in subtle ways, in a language that we cannot hear. We never see a flock of birds crashing into each other when flying in formation. Each bird seems to uncannily know when and where to turn, or perhaps they talk to each other in a language we humans don't hear. In India, people believe that a pet cat or a dog can sense imminent death in a family and may cry or make strange sounds to indicate danger. One famous feline, Oscar, who lives in a Providence, Rhode Island, nursing home, can unerringly determine when a patient is about to die. Normally antisocial, he gravitates to the bed of the dying one, where he cuddles up.

According to the US Geological Survey anecdotal evidence abounds of animals, fish, birds, reptiles, and insects exhibiting strange behavior anywhere from weeks to seconds before an earthquake. The agency's website says that mechanisms have not been discovered to explain how animals could sense quakes days or weeks before they happen.

Plants too are stunningly aware! Many other researchers have determined beyond all doubt that plants also respond to our love and positive vibrations. If we talk to a plant that is dying, if we touch it lovingly, it may revive and recover. Conversely, if we think about inflicting harm, as when we contemplate the weeds in our garden, the targeted weeds quake, and communicate their distress to the other plants, aware of their death sentence.

These examples indeed suggest that a discrete form of communication exists among all living beings. And the common thread underlying this is energy.

All living beings are basically energy, at one intensity or another. It is like air—it is all around us and in us but we cannot see it, even though we know that it's there. We are all connected through this energy with all other living beings. Experts say that telepathy works on the basis of energy transmitted, or perhaps instantly and non-locally shared, between people. People living at a similar vibration of energy are able to communicate easily with one another; one person thinks and the other person catches the thought and understands. They also call this "chemistry" between people. Ironically, while some people can communicate across vast distances in elegant silence, there are others who, despite loudly spoken words during an argument, are unable to get their point across.

A question that arises then is, can this chemistry be developed between people, or between other living beings? Can beings tune up their energy levels to be able to communicate with one another in a mutually harmonious way, like the notes of various musical instruments producing music in an orchestra?

Energy vibrates at different frequencies in all living beings. This can be especially evident at the human level, where energy vibrations fluctuate with our spiritual state. The lower our energy vibration is, the "farther away" we are from True Source, and the more animalistic or negative qualities we will demonstrate. It is natural law that we will encounter more negative people and situations of a similar vibration.

Conversely, the higher the frequency of our energy vibrations, the closer we are to True Source. Our constitution becomes subtler. At these vibrations, we attract experiences and people of similar frequency. It is for this reason that whenever I come into the presence of a spiritual person, I can immediately sense a calming influence. Their energy levels are palpable. In the same way, there have been times when I have felt distinctly uncomfortable when coming into the presence of unknown people, without a word being spoken, for reasons I have not been able to pin down.

I remember one incident when my husband was traveling in a taxi in India. It was drizzling and the open car window would not shut, so he moved to the other side of the car. Shortly after that, another car hit the taxi on the side where my husband had been sitting earlier. Because he had moved to the other side, he escaped injury. You might call this a coincidence. I understood this to be a demonstration of the energy principle. I believe that he must have been at a higher vibration that time, and hence was able to avoid the accident.

We can increase or decrease the frequency of vibrations at which we live and work. Yes, we can tune up our energy levels to align with our soul, by changing the way we think and the way we act, by developing the qualities of the soul and bringing them to life. This can be realized by living in faith and gratitude, by positive thinking, by choosing to live consciously and, above all, by our compassion for all forms of life, and for ourselves.

This may seem like a tall order, but it really isn't. Yes, we do have the power to control our energy levels, simply by making the right choices.

It *is* all in our hands. The thing is, we are not aware of this, or if we are, we often don't want to make the effort. It is easier to blame others, society, and even our destiny, than to take responsibility for our actions. We like to absolve ourselves of responsibility toward ourselves to evolve as spiritual beings. It seems easier to wallow in worldly pleasures and pains than to explore our inner world. We get caught up in day-to-day chores and entertainments, and do not give enough time and thought to this essential aspect of our life.

It is not difficult to raise our energy levels. There is no miracle or rocket science in this. We can all do it just by *changing the way we live.* This is about making spirituality a way of life, which is different from unthinking adherence to religious dogma and rituals.

In a truly spiritual life, nothing is forced on us. Nobody sits in judgment, punishing us for our so-called wrongdoings. We ourselves shape our experiences with our thoughts and actions. Those able to work in harmony with their life's spiritual purpose, and who have learnt to create a beautiful life by fine-tuning their energy levels, would experience what some call "heaven on earth." By the same token, life is difficult for those who have gravitated toward negativity and darkness, and who live devoid of love, compassion, and a connection to their own inner world. Their life can be a "living hell."

To my way of thinking, this range in vibrations explains the existence of all kinds of experiences in our world, from agony to ecstasy. Once we understand the *Real Truth,* and start raising our energy levels by fine – tuning to the needs of our soul, material things and worldly recognition lose their importance. Then all that really matters is our connection with the Divine. Nothing else is important. Absolutely *no-thing.*

My Reflections

....

....

....

....

....

....

....

....

....

....

....

....

....

....

....

....

....

....

41

Is spirituality compatible with practical living?

"Be in the world, do not ignore it. Spirituality does not have to mean finding a cave and hiding out forever. Be in your world but not of it. Remember that the world was created for you so that you might have a context within which to experience yourself as Who You Really Are."

Neale Donald Walsch

The quest for spiritual awakening sometimes requires profound changes in one's lifestyle. There are some who argue that strict and religious adherence to particular rules of conduct is essential. Others suggest that a complete withdrawal from worldly thoughts and affairs is prerequisite to spiritual progress. Another common belief is that living a spiritual life is not entirely compatible with normal day-to-day life. Nevertheless, many can easily abide by spiritual values in a practical way in their lives.

After my awakening, it became apparent that all of us could lead a spiritual life as ordinary people, simply by changing *the way* we live. We need not leave our home and family to sit in a remote Himalayan cave or ashram to follow our spiritual calling.

In India, one often meets people who live secluded and ascetic lives, with minimal or no involvement in matters of career and family. They go through penance and brave the challenges of nature. Finding it easier to contemplate the Divine in solitude, they usually isolate themselves from worldly affairs with a deep sense of detachment from the "external." By withdrawing from the world, they effectively cut themselves off from stimuli that could distract their minds and spark more thoughts. The mind is thus freed for contemplation and meditation. The incentive in detachment is the hope that it will encourage conscious unity with the Divine. In this way, they are totally divorced from issues that many of us choose to deal with in our lives. This is their spiritual calling, a different stage of spiritual evolution.

Each one of us has an individual spiritual path, and the time and experiences for each one's journey are unique. For some, the process of spiritual enquiry starts early in life, and for no apparent reason. Others make this change, from a worldly life to a more inward one, midway through their lives. They are called to abandon the worldly life for a life of contemplation. This can be traumatic and challenging for them, as well as for their families.

A few years back I met a charming lady who made this transition late in her adult life. A god-fearing and religious person, she lived a modest life with her husband and children. At some stage she took a dramatic step of walking away from her apparently happy urban life. She chose to leave her husband and two teenage children to go and live in an ashram in India, to follow her "calling." She started her life anew with others, who had similarly given up their families to lead what they took to be a more spiritual life of prayer and serving the poor in the neighborhood. I recall wondering at that time how emotionally challenging it must have been for her to take such a drastic step. Quite possibly, this would have been traumatic for her family.

I hear of others who have had very traumatic personal experiences before they reach the threshold of spiritual awakening. These may be experiences of severe physical illnesses or personal trauma that make them realize the futility of ego driven lives and make them search for something deeper.

What creates the tipping point for each person is a mystery to me. The answer probably goes back to the temple priest many years back who advised me of individual spiritual journeys. I do not believe that we necessarily need to go through painful experiences to awaken to truth or to make decisive shifts in awareness. I am drawn to the idea of a spiritual life wherein people lead their "normal" lives, facing day-to-day challenges—struggles for work and income, child needs, health problems, relationship issues in the family—and still live with a shift in *awareness.*

To me, spirituality is a way of life without relinquishment of duties or abandonment of emotional ties. Facing these realities squarely affords us the opportunity to evolve spiritually. It challenges us to experience life without letting our ego intervene. It makes us aware of limiting thought patterns and of the need to break them. It allows us to fully feel our feelings and to understand where healing needs to take place inside us. It brings to our awareness the attitude we need to make the shift inwards. In all of these openings, reasons for gratitude to the Divine Source shine more and more brightly. We then get a sharper sense of our spiritual growth. What we need to do is *open up* to receiving grace and to stay *awake!* In the present moment, there is neither the time nor the space for emotional baggage and blockages. Soul qualities come NOW to the fore, and we start making conscious and spontaneously harmonious choices about this life.

The theme of detaching from worldly entanglements as a key step toward spiritual enlightenment occurs frequently in Hindu scriptures. The logic for this has been compellingly presented to me in some interesting spiritual discourses that I have attended. However, I feel that the process can also be completely natural. When we get *attached* to the Divine to start with, for all that He has blessed us with, and live in His prayers, detachment from the material life occurs spontaneously. We do not have to make an attempt. It is a normal transition to a stage in which the material world loses its importance as our connection to the *True Source* strengthens. In this way, gratitude and faith beget detachment.

In my case, as I have grown spiritually, the more I experience my inner connection to the Divine, and the less my interest in shopping (my husband loves this!) and in accumulation of material possessions. I have chosen not to stop caring for my family and my duties toward them. I have not stopped going on an occasional holiday nor do I avoid meeting people. But I feel a clear difference in the way that I relate to people and deal with issues in my life.

I live my practical life with a sense of detachment. I do whatever is required but I am at the same time detached emotionally from events and results. There is now an internal equanimity that does not get disturbed, even when outside stimuli change. How to live in this world and enjoy everything that the Divine has given us—without getting attached to anything—is the meaning of spirituality that I understand. This shift in perspective is indeed very humbling and joyful.

To achieve anything, we need to have three things—knowledge, action, and focus. We have to have the knowledge and skills required; we need to execute our plans, and we need to maintain focus to achieve what we want. Whenever we apply these three attributes to any action in a positive way, we can get the results we seek. However, for any action to be spiritual, there must be one additional element: the action has to be not for *me* or *my,* but for the manifestation of the highest good. The determining factor as to the merit of an action is our intention behind what we do. Actions undertaken mainly for personal gain keep us firmly anchored at the worldly level. Ego-driven, they lose what might otherwise have communicated sacredness and beauty. Such calculated action can keep us attached, and only hold us back spiritually, rather than taking us forward.

The door remains always open for spiritual awareness to enter into even the most mundane activities. I believe that when this approach evolves into a merger between the two, we can perform any role in life successfully. All roles thus become spiritual expressions, simply by changing our attitude regarding "ends," and the means to those ends.

I truly understood the meaning of detachment in regard to the results of my actions after I *woke up.* Along with this came the realization that we need to accept as blessings and grace from the Divine whatever results we get. Only by complete surrender and grateful acceptance of "what is" can we be truly spiritual. That is my conviction.

My Reflections

....
....
....
....
....
....
....
....
....
....
....
....
....
....
....
....
....
....
....
....
....
....

42
Our life's purpose

*"As human beings we all want to be happy and free from misery…
we have learned that the key to happiness is inner peace. The
greatest obstacles to inner peace are disturbing emotions such as
anger, attachment, fear and suspicion, while love and compassion
and a sense of universal responsibility are the sources of peace and
happiness."*

Dalai Lama

Some of us spend much of our life not thinking about spiritual matters. Preoccupation with practical challenges may keep us away from deeper reflection about our life and our being. When some of us do delve deeper into spirituality, one question often confounds us: What, after all is said and done, is the purpose of this life? Why am I here? This question has often perplexed me as well.

In exploring this question, I start by proposing that each life does have a larger purpose. As we move forward in our life and reflect upon our life's journey, each experience begins to make sense, complementing all the others perfectly. This can be true with respect to all our experiences, pleasant as well as unpleasant.

When we watch a movie, we see so many characters coming and going. We may not understand their role initially when they are introduced.

They perform their assigned roles and fade away. As the action unfolds, we reflect back on all the characters and dialogues. We then understand how each one fit into the story line. Gradually, all the roles, situations, and events fall into place and we get the full picture.

Our life is like a movie too. We relate to many different characters; we go through a wealth of experiences – some positive and some negative, some pleasant and some painful. And as our life story plays out, we may not immediately understand how each friend or family member has been filling a necessary role, helping to shape our personality and make us the way we are. As we reflect on some key events and trends, the "story line" of our life can begin to look clearer. Our view of many events and people is likely to change, and what had appeared to be mere coincidence could then be recognized as Divine design. Our understanding can grow dramatically.

In the case of a movie, the director knows the entire plot, and the actors look to him to vividly spin their tale. In "real life," the Universe is the movie director. It knows exactly what will happen before we do. It is then up to us to get that larger perspective, to see how the script of our life develops. One way to do this is to see it exactly as we would watch a movie—as an observer.

As I look back on my childhood, I can see myself gradually learning basic life skills as I grew up. Considering the challenges that I faced, my failures and successes, and I say, yes, I learnt something there. I have seen some of my dreams realized and others not. I have grown from each such experience and moved on. My life makes more sense now.

At the spiritual level, at the level of the soul, similar dynamics are at work. In each life we have opportunities to adapt, to evolve, and to learn our lessons. The trick here is that if we do *not* look at the mix of life experiences from a spiritual perspective, we will miss the larger picture.

We are all born at a particular time and place, and into circumstances that our soul chooses. This choice is made to give us those experiences that are conducive to bringing us back to True Source, spiritually enriched. As we go through those experiences, it is upon us to learn from them at the spiritual level so that we can move on.

While the circumstances of our life are our soul's choice, how we utilize them in a spiritual context is our choice. In the words of Swami Chinmayananda, "What you have is God's gift to you; what you do with what you have is your gift to Him." All experiences in life are meant to help us develop qualities of the soul, to show us how to love, how to be compassionate, humble, and forgiving.

How then do we reconcile the power of choice and the Grand design of the Universe? The answer to this question is to understand that the Big He has a plan, and enables and empowers us at the small He level to make the choices that are in our best interest and in line with the plan. Eventually all small He's will evolve spiritually to merge into the Big He. Therefore, it is upon us to make the choices that can move us into that direction.

We have all been given a chance to grow and develop our soul qualities, but all too often we do not make time to still our mind and look at the patterns that have come into our life. We tend not to think about why we've had a particular experience, and what spiritual lessons it may have offered.

We say we have no time to think as we run through our lives, let alone pursue spiritual interests. But we actually don't need time to be compassionate and loving, to feel grateful for our blessings, to develop the qualities of our soul. After all, to be kind and compassionate all we need is our connection to the Divine Source. We are born with these qualities, but we tend to lose them over time. The Universe has its ways of regularly reminding us of this. Our instincts on these matters are by nature very strong when we are closer to the Divine. But people who do not listen to their inner voice end up deaf to the voice of their conscience. They keep snubbing its promptings, and because they overlook it every time it gives a message, they lose it altogether.

It has been said, originally by French philosopher Teilhard de Chardin, that we are not human beings having a spiritual experience, but spiritual beings having a human experience. Spiritual knowledge is not arcane or inaccessible, nor is it separate from us. It is our very essence. The True Source has made this knowledge available to us, but it behooves us to rediscover it, become aware of it, and live it in this very lifetime. It is not some "thing" you "do" for an hour a day. You do not simply listen to, or read words about it. It is not like knowledge that you talk about and discuss and then store away at the back of your head. It is an experience in itself. It has to be applied, to be experienced as the essence of your being, animating your every breath. It has to be absorbed by every cell in the body so that it cleanses and changes the way you live. Spirituality has to be lived, not performed, as one of the routine activities in life. It cannot and should not be separated from all the worldly roles we play in our everyday life.

I now understand and believe that this is the larger purpose to life, a bigger picture that eventually unfolds before us, and the question no longer confounds me. Every experience in life is meant to help us to move toward that larger purpose. Once we have that faith in our Divine Plan, a faith that comes with spiritual awareness, we will automatically welcome all experiences, good or bad, and use them as opportunities to help evolve our soul.

My Reflections

....

....

....

....

....

....

....

....

....

....

....

....

....

....

....

....

....

....

....

Part Eight

STAYING AWAKE, BEING ALIVE

Continuing Our Spiritual Journey

43

Continuing our spiritual journey

"You are awareness. Awareness is another name for you. Since you are awareness there is no need to attain or cultivate it. All that you have to do is to give up being aware of other thing, that is of the not-Self. If one gives up being aware of them then pure awareness alone remains, and that is the Self."

Ramana Maharshi

A discussion of the Soul, its qualities and its evolution, naturally raises a further question: Where does the individual soul come from, and how does it relate to the larger "entity" or Divine Source that most faiths refer to? And what qualities could we associate with this Divine Source?

Although different religions have assigned specific deferential names to their chosen God, contemporary spiritual writers have used a range of generic terms to refer to the Divine Source: God, True Source, the Universe, the Real Truth, Source, The One, Presence, and so on. During my Reiki sessions, I found myself relating better to the term *Energy* to represent the Divine Source. I understood this term to best represent what I feel about the Divine Source, i.e., a vast, limitless reservoir of energy that comprises this Universe. It cannot be visualized but it permeates everything and every being; it is everywhere, like the air in and around us. We don't see it, but we *know* it is everywhere. And at the individual level, we are a quantum of the same energy. We are a part of it, we emanate from it and are formed of the same substance.

In Vedanta, a philosophy based on Hindu sacred scriptures, there is an interesting analogy for this relationship between the Infinite Source and the individual. It is said that just as individual waves in an ocean arise from the ocean and fall back into it, individual lives arise out of the infinite Divine Source, are contained for a while in the vessel of a body, and then merge back into the same Source. Essentially, there is no difference between the substance of the waves and the ocean. They both consist of the same water. However, the wave has a finite experience, whereas the ocean represents the Infinite Source.

When we are born as individual souls, we come with the same qualities as the Divine Source—love, compassion, kindness, peace, and joy. Throughout life, when we experience or encounter these qualities, we know we like them. They give us an ultimate kind of joy. Yet many of us are not able to sustain these feelings; we seem to lose this state as we move along in life.

Why do we often feel miserable and suffer when it is our real nature to be in joy and in peace? Why are we looking for happiness outside and not inside of ourselves? Why do we have low self-esteem issues and insecurities? Why are we looking for external power to feel complete when we are infused with the energy of love? Why do we allow a strong ego to run our lives when humility is our real nature?

The irony is that we start with a clean slate as a newborn, but as we go through life, our attention moves farther and farther away from our spiritual essence. In fact, we ourselves develop a whole range of obstacles to impede our spiritual growth. We develop insecurities and lose our self-esteem. Then, to feel worthy and complete, we scramble after external power. The more beautiful, wealthy, and knowledgeable we become, the more complete we feel—at least temporarily. In the process, mind and ego take control of our lives. We start losing ourselves in the material plane. We lose touch with our inner self. We forget our connection with all living beings. We see others and ourselves as entirely discrete entities, not as part of the same ocean. Emotional blockages start building up and feed on each other, depleting us of our ability to love unconditionally.

Resentments of the past, negative emotions, fears of the future—all combine to sully and coarsen our energy levels, increasing density and heaviness. Like the sticky and heavy oil molecules that foul our seas and stay separate from the water, our negativities contaminate us; our dense and polluted energy levels take us away from awareness of the True Source.

The heavier our energy becomes, the farther we seem to be from True Source, which is light and pure. Having lost touch with the spiritual qualities of our individual soul, we may feel in many ways "detached" from our Source. You'll remember, however, that in the analogy of the ocean, the wave remains connected to the ocean at all times. It may feel itself to have a distinct existence, but it does not detach.

That is why the remembrance of the Divine Source requires that we fully recognize our soul qualities. This becomes the purpose of our life, as we discussed earlier. Only when droplets of oil are slowly diluted and cleansed can we see and feel pure water. Similarly, to become cleaner and purer, to remember our connection to the True Source, we need to "decontaminate," cleanse and energetically lighten ourselves.

Our thoughts are energy, too. That is why thoughts have such great power to either take awareness away from, or bring it closer to True Source. Positive thoughts will attract only positive energy vibrations. Negative thoughts will attract only negative consequences to match that energy vibration. By redirecting our fears to thoughts of love, we can experience greater closeness to our True Source. Thoughts thus become the way to our realization of Oneness.

Clearing the past baggage that has clogged us can lighten our energy levels. We need to release our negativities. Only when we are able to quiet our mind and be still can we feel the presence of True Source within us. Stopping the chatter in our minds and focusing on the *now* can help us release blockages and open to our Source. Living in gratitude is especially helpful in unclogging the channels. Prayers offered with faith and purity of mind, rather than desperation and expectation, can help us release the blockages.

Once we have recognized the qualities of the soul and understand that they are what we need to abide in our True Source, we have taken a key step on our spiritual journey. Experiencing these qualities in this life, feeling them deep within, leads to ever-increasing wakefulness, and life takes a different turn. That is when love and compassion become second nature; that is when forgiveness and humility come naturally. Prayer and gratitude then come from the heart, and faith in the running of the Universe is so central and profound that all experiences have a spiritual meaning. That is when we understand the difference between spiritual knowledge and spiritual experience. That is when we understand that no words can express this sacred experience.

And that is when life becomes beautiful and we can start living "in joy." Lighting our lamp within in this manner, we begin to awaken and truly live.

My Reflections